Narcissistic Giving:

A Study of People Who Cheat in Relationships

Gerald Alper

Narcissistic Giving:

A Study of People Who Cheat in Relationships

Gerald Alper

Austin & Winfield, Publishers
San Francisco-London-Bethesda, 1995

Library of Congress Cataloging-in-Publication Data

Alper, Gerald.
  Narcissistic giving : or why it seems relationships never work / Gerald
Alper.
        p. cm.
  Includes bibliographical references and index.
  ISBN 1-883255-80-5: $29.95.-- ISBN 1-883255-81-3 (pbk.): $19.95
    1. Narcissism. 2. Artists--Psychology. 3. Interpersonal relations.
    4. Intimacy (Psychology) I. Title.
BF575.N35A47 1995
158'.2--dc20   94-28831
                                                       CIP

Copyright 1995 by

Editorial Inquiries:
International Scholars Publications
7831 Woodmont Avenue #345
Bethesda,MD.20814

To order: (800) 55-PUBLISH

For Anita
who, more than anyone else, helped me
to recognize and to better understand (in her words)
"the preciousness of the true self and the
unnecessary destructiveness of deception".

TABLE OF CONTENTS

Preface

Recently, a friend and a colleague, a professional psychotherapist who had just published a book which I myself considered brilliant, was complaining about what he viewed as ill treatment and neglect at the hands of his publisher. Compounding the complaint was the fact that he could not pinpoint the source of his dissatisfaction. He just knew that whenever he spoke to anyone engaged in some facet of publishing his book -- whether in marketing, distributing, selling or publicizing it -- he invariably came away from the conversation feeling that he had been somehow politely but efficiently dismissed. Not just in the overall, but even in the highly particular scheme of things pertaining to his own work where you would have thought his individual expertise would have counted for something. Not so. Instead, it was as though there were a machine, a technology or established method, faithfully adhered to, which superseded the random or collective impact of mere authors.

Things came to a head in the mind of my friend when he was apprised, three months after publication, that the first quarter sales figures were surprisingly low. Confident that the book was good and armed with a bevy of glowing advance reviews, he suddenly became anxious that he was not receiving even the minimal support he needed from his publisher, and that perhaps, for reasons unfathomable to him, a premature decision had been covertly made to write him off. To reassure himself this was not the case, he sought out the publicist and respectfully but pointedly inquired as to the nature and extent of the efforts that were being carried out on behalf of his book. He was made to feel (or so it seemed to him) that he was being a bit obsessive, as the publicist -- a hearty woman who fielded his questions with ease -- ended their conversation by reminding him that she had "been doing publicity for years."

It was this phrase, especially, which he could not swallow, and could not understand why he could not swallow it; and it was the juncture at which I intervened, saying simply, "No wonder, she didn't give you anything."

Seeing that I had indeed captured his attention, I proceeded to quickly analyze the interaction as an instance of something I was in the habit of calling *narcissistic giving*, examples of which I had been steadfastly accumulating for years. Expanding on what I had said (hoping it might afford my friend a measure of relief) I pointed out just how well that brief phrase encapsulated months of frustrating interactions between himself and his publisher and I encouraged him to look more seriously at the true meaning of those innocent words, "been doing publicity for years." On the one hand, it offered the gift of reassurance (which is really what had been asked for in the first place), that there was no need to worry, that everything that had to be done, that should be done, was being done. After all, the tone seemed to imply, how could someone who had been doing this for years, do anything less? Yet, on the other hand, there was the undeniable let down, the lingering feeling that little, if anything, had been resolved.

It was this latter perception that contained, so I believed, the crux of my friend's malaise. For what, exactly, had been given or accomplished from the standpoint of his needs? By his own testimony, he was disheartened by the unexpectedly meager sales of a book he had labored long and hard to produce. Insidiously, he had become frightened, perhaps even paranoid, that he had been somehow lost in the shuffle, that he was small potatoes, not even worthy of the backing of his own publisher. For months he had had the unsettling impression that the people he was speaking to were doing so only because they had to, and that there were far more important things to which they would rather address their energies. So, when he finally did screw up his courage and confront his publicist, it was in order to find out some specific, urgently needed information. He wanted to know, among other things, if his apprehensions were correct that he was not being adequately promoted, and if that were the case, did it mean it was because he was not respected, and did that in turn suggest he had made a terrible mistake in trusting his publisher in the first place?

Seen this way, in the light of such mounting uneasiness which could not help but come through, the publicist's words seemed incredibly deficient. Upon examination, the publicist's so-called gift of reassurance came to nothing more than an affirmation of her experience and accumulated expertise. By thereby focusing exclusively on her resumé rather than on the quality of her service, attention was automatically deflected from the paucity of what was presumably being given.

To put it plainly but not unfairly, the publicist's gift, especially from the context of what was being asked, was worthless and this was not because it was an isolated, aberrant or incidental occurrence. On the contrary, when the narcissistic giving element is linked to the ownership of allegedly legitimatized qualifications, it is a measure of just how enamored our culture is with hierarchy, status and power that someone in evident need (such as my friend) will often be satisfied, or at least disarmed, with nothing more than a recitation of one's credentials. And the higher one moves up the professional ladder, the truer this is. So that if, for example, one is a medical doctor, it becomes almost possible to answer many questions by merely reminding someone, especially someone in a subservient position, of the fact that one is a doctor: i.e. that one is a certified expert, but that the other is *not*.

From such an interaction (an expert who sees fit to brandish his expertise without exercising it) certain abuses imperceptibly follow. Perhaps foremost is that between the expert-giver and the designated recipient, a false self relationship is set up. A false self relationship is one in which no real exchange, communication or contact between the true selves of either party is allowed to take place. This is almost guaranteed to occur once the putative expert behaves in such a way as to indicate that the status of expect confers special rights and privileges, and carries with it an implicit corresponding expectation of the other that there will be the proper respect and confirmation for the manifestly unequal relationship. This inequity of prestige can be so great that the message is sometimes given that the other should be grateful for just being permitted to come into close proximity with such superior skill. The implication is therefore that by being allowed to enter the sphere of influence of the expert, a gift has been bestowed and a beneficiary has been appointed. Here, perhaps, an unconscious analogy is operating between the impact of the authority figure and that of the celebrity, (where there is no longer any pretense of giving the audience anything more than a presence). However, when it is the expert (as in the case of my friend's publicist) who acts this way, who, instead of providing the professional service for which she has been paid, retreats from authentic giving (i.e. the deliverance of what has been basically promised) and points to what might be called the charisma of her credentials ("I've been doing publicity for years") narcissistic giving takes place.

Narcissistic giving may be defined as a defense against the anxiety of being exposed as someone with an impaired capacity to nurture the interpersonal needs of another -- by pretending that one is not only giving enough, but is giving more than enough, in fact, is giving gratuitously. The story of my friend, who, demoralized by surprisingly dismal sales figures for a book that had been ten years in the making, went to his publicist in the hope of obtaining useful information and, perhaps, realistic consolation and received instead only a cheerful reminder that she, in effect, knew her stuff -- was an example of narcissistic giving.

There are numerous opportunities for such an interaction to spontaneously arise in the business and professional world. When it does, the prospects for developing a nurturing relationship, one in which trust is mutually given and earned, are seriously undermined. A deleterious side effect of a relationship with an expert which has narcissistic giving at its core is that the so-called beneficiary not only does not receive the expected benefit, but typically goes away feeling bad about himself (as was certainly the case with my friend): i.e., there is the realization on some level that one has shamefully allowed oneself to be unnecessarily intimidated by the mantle of authority into callously pretending that the narcissistic giving has been something more, something of value.

No one has to tell me after spending nearly ten years in an assortment of therapeutic and analytic training institutes, how difficult it is to question the prevailing mystique of the powers that be, and to call a spade a spade. When it comes to the prescribed code of professional behavior by which prospective therapists are instructed to treat future patients, such an authoritarian overview, if unchecked, can lead to something I have called *technique as narcissistic giving*: i.e. the grandiose belief on the part of the therapist that the application of correct technique -- regardless of its particular impact on the individual patient -- can somehow by itself be an agent of beneficial change, and at its best, even something that transcends the cure for which it was designed.

Perhaps nowhere else is this more self-evident than in the case of the single session consultation visit, where the focus of the expectant patient is understandably almost entirely on appraising the professional credentials of the alleged expert. In such circumstances, as I have written elsewhere, it is unfortunately almost standard practice for the consulting psychotherapist -- in light of the fact that an economic boost from a potential new patient is tantalizingly in the offing -- to devote the brunt of his energy to a no-risk demonstration that he is in possession of whatever technique, or suite of techniques, he considers his strong suit. Let us say he is successful in this endeavor and convinces the prospective patient that he is qualified to treat him. Let us further imagine that the prospective patient unconsciously colludes by persuading himself that something important has thereby just happened, he has met someone who is capable of helping him.

What is typically overlooked by both parties in such a familiar scenario is that a relationship between two people has been set up which almost guarantees -- if the initial premise upon which it has been founded is adhered to -- that nothing of import can occur. For what good does it do to a patient if someone has just demonstrated that he knows something, but has not imparted anything of what he knows? In this regard, what is true of the teacher is true of the therapist -- it is not so much what he knows, but what he can facilitate someone else to learn. Just as far too many teachers are satisfied if they are merely teaching well, so are far too many therapists content if they are simply managing to come across as expert-like -- so that they never really get to the key point of determining whether the patient is absorbing whatever it is they believe they are giving.

Compounding all of this is the fact that the other side of the coin of narcissistic giving is narcissistic injury. This is because: since narcissistic giving is a grandiose defense against a lingering suspicion that one has little of true substance or nurturance to give, there will be an understandable touchiness, even paranoia, about eventually being exposed. And to the narcissistic giver -- unable to admit the underlying fragility of his lavish pose -- such exposure can only seem persecutory. After all, if he is really giving far more than is required (in this case, the gift of his expertise or technique as narcissistic giving) and is still being rejected -- then it can only be because nothing he will ever do will be respected. It is easy to see when this is the case, the response is often a paranoia-induced narcissistic injury.

When a narcissistic injury of this type is incurred by a putative expert, someone invested with considerable social and professional power, the instinctive reaction can be the polar opposite of an honest reparative attempt to communicate the hurt in the hope of redressing it. Instead, there may be a vindictive drive to burnish a tarnished image by reestablishing the traditional power gulf between expert and non-expert (e.g., putting the person in his place); or even, when there is a sadistic need to create the greatest possible separation of roles, to employ the tactic of expert humiliation (e.g., throwing one's credentials in someone's face).

An example, culled from my private practice as a psychotherapist in New York City, related to me in vivid detail by Sarah, a supervisee, and one of the best psychotherapists I had ever worked with, nicely illustrates this:

It concerned one of Sarah's patients whom she had encouraged -- because of episodic suicidal fantasies -- to seek out a psychiatric consultation in order to explore the need for anti-depressants. Accordingly, the patient had arranged for a visit with a psychiatrist; but first she had made it clear on the telephone that she already had a psychotherapist (Sarah) and was therefore only looking for, at most, someone who might monitor her medication if such was required. When the psychiatrist responded, "That's all right. It can only be for medication. Of course, if after meeting me, you'd like to talk to me, that would be all right, too." -- she became suspicious.

Her suspicion was reinforced during the ensuing consultation session, as she became increasingly uncomfortable at what seemed to her the psychiatrist's peculiar habit of periodically interrupting his own history taking to inquire, "And what did your therapist say?" The patient, who to begin with was hypersensitive to any real or imagined criticism of anything pertaining to her own judgments (which certainly included her choice of psychotherapists), found herself in the embarrassing position of having to protect her therapist. As the session progressed, she became increasingly paranoid: first, over whether Sarah was being judiciously appraised, or really being secretly discredited, and, then, whether it was her own way of managing things, her very lifestyle, which -- under the smoke screen of a medical history taking -- was being superciliously critiqued. Such ruminations quickly undermined her, having the effect of transforming in her mind what should have been a routine psychiatric examination into a devious and unnerving cross-examination. So, when she reported (as was true) that she had experimented with the then new wonder drug, Prosac, (under prescription from a previous psychiatrist) and had suffered as a side effect a type of hallucination which she had never before experienced and the psychiatrist had dismissively responded, "I've never heard that before" -- she brashly shot back, "You're hearing it now."

Convinced now that the psychiatrist respected neither her therapist nor herself, she went from being defensive to being defiant. When the psychiatrist -- noting her mounting touchiness, especially on the subject of her therapist's background -- pointed out that he needed to ask such questions because, after all, he did not know and had never heard of Sarah, she snapped, "Sarah hasn't heard of you either!" And, finally, when, submitting to his persistence, she had responded in exasperation that Sarah's orientation, so far as she knew, was that of psychoanalytic psychotherapist and the psychiatrist had seemingly proclaimed triumphantly, "So you see, she's *not* a doctor!" -- it was more than she could bear. Putting herself down was one thing, but putting down someone upon whom she depended, was something else.

Deciding that her therapist had been not only bested but devalued, she became demoralized. The fight drained out of her, and she lost even her customary willingness to defensively assert herself. When the consulting psychiatrist observed and commented on her noticeable withdrawal ("you seem depressed"), she reacted as though she had been branded rather than diagnosed. This time, though, she hid her feelings until the session had ended and she had safely arrived home. There in the privacy of her bedroom, where there was no one before whom she needed to put up a brave front, she did what she always did when she felt humiliated: she cried for hours.

When she next saw Sarah, not surprisingly, she spent the entire session chronicling how what was supposed to have been a benign psychiatric consultation had turned into (as she saw it) a lesson in degradation. Although Sarah was well aware of her patient's hypersensitivity to perceived criticism and her tendency to overreact with provocative bravado, she also trusted her patient's social judgment enough to become professionally concerned and alerted to the possibility that subtle abuse (which could never, of course, be proven) had in fact occurred. And when this same consulting psychiatrist telephoned her not once but several times in the course of the following week (presumably to report his findings and to exchange professional information) Sarah listened intently, not only from the standpoint of what he had to say about her patient, but especially in light of what his words might tell her about his true intention and underlying attitude toward her patient. After three such telephone calls in a row -- with the psychiatrist becoming appreciably anxious as he realized he was never going to see this particular referral again -- Sarah became convinced (as I did upon hearing her account) that her patient's perceptions had been on target: the doctor indeed had been primarily invested in salvaging as many additional referral sessions as he could and was prepared to be blatantly manipulative if that is what it took.

Although such behavior is extreme, it is a not uncommon example of the abuse that can follow when an expert (in this instance, a consulting psychiatrist, but it could as easily have been a psychotherapist, a medical doctor, or any other kind of self-proclaimed or licensed specialist) -- instead of generously delivering the advertised service -- under the shelter of narcissistic giving, covertly aspires to gratify purely selfish aims.

When that happens, a painful, typically negative lesson is learned, e.g. Sarah's patient realizing, to her horror, that the psychiatrist she had visited was more interested in procuring a new source of revenue than in creating a benign consulting relationship which might supply the necessary data to construct a useful psychiatric diagnosis and a timely prescription for medication. Perhaps even more damaging was what transpired when she challenged what she saw as his spurious professionalism (playing oneupmanship with his medical credentials) and he responded, chiefly, by becoming narcissistically injured: by (1) grandiosely asserting, "So Sarah is not a doctor!," and (2) using his power to retaliate, "You're depressed!"

The demoralization shown by Sarah's patient -- who alternated between depression and pseudo bravado -- is a frequent outcome to such narcissistic giving for someone who is fragile to begin with, but it is by no means restricted to oversensitive patients. In general, on a lesser scale, there is always disappointment, a sense (often unconscious) that one has somehow been shortchanged, when one is subjected to narcissistic giving. Regarding the example at hand, from my own experience, on the few occasions when I sought out a consultation visit from a psychotherapist, I could not help but be impressed (and therefore disappointed) with the degree to which even highly recommended and supposedly well qualified professionals labored to cover their tracks and to come across as error-free role models of mental health in their self-centered quest to gain a new patient. Now, while there is nothing wrong with wanting a new patient, what is thereby most forgotten is what is most obvious: that the point of a consultation is not to satisfy the needs of a therapist to secure an additional referral, but to satisfy the needs of the patient which essentially are to learn as much as possible in the allotted time so as to determine whether it makes sense to make a contract of sorts with the professional one is seeing for the very first time.

To arrive at such an important decision is difficult enough, even when the therapist is fully cooperating, doing his best to disclose who he is professionally so that the prospective patient will have as clear an idea as possible at this initial stage of what he or she might be in for later on. Some of the things the patient particularly wants to know are: what kind of person is the therapist, really, how giving, kind, nurturing, genuinely interested in improving his or her psychological situation is he as opposed to economically using it for a profit?, and what depth and breadth of therapeutic life experience and interpretative, empathic resonance will he be able to offer? In other words, what is most necessary in order to meet the needs of the patient is for the therapist -- not to perform -- but to *show* who he is professionally (without gratifying, colluding, or overpromising).   In this light, it is easy to see that narcissistic giving does the exact opposite: it allows the self-interested expert to complacently hide behind the mantle of institutionalized, supposedly impeccable credentials and to deceive himself into believing that by simply brandishing his expertise he has somehow discharged his responsibility and given something of value. And viewed this way, the pain and subsequent sobbing of Sarah's patient, become illuminated as being by no means solely attributable to her hypersensitivity and proclivity to perceive people, especially authority figures, as critically persecuting her. On the contrary, when it is seen that her perception of her consulting psychiatrist as being primarily self-motivated was quite real (as both Sarah and I had to agree) it became understandable why she was so devastated. Part of the damaging aftermath of narcissistic giving -- although often an unintended side effect of a person who is exclusively and blindly intent upon gratifying pressing, largely unconscious aims -- is rooted in the fact that unfortunately it works best when its target happens to be someone who is particularly needy and vulnerable (as was certainly the case with my friend who was so disheartened by the inexplicably dismal sales figures reported for his book and with Sarah's patient, who, characteristically ill at ease in the presence of a strange psychiatrist, required some definite reassurance).

This is because someone who is needy is naturally susceptible to being persuaded that another person may have an answer of sorts to the dilemma at hand: i.e., the threshold of belief that gratification is plausibly in the offing sharply drops. To the degree that one becomes convinced one is about to be given to, expectation will quickly be aroused; while on the other hand, to the extent that the anticipated gratification does not pan out (as it never does when narcissistic giving is operative) a proportionate disappointment will as swiftly take hold.

It is therefore not surprising that people who have been on the receiving end of narcissistic giving (e.g., Sarah's patient) are often convinced -- in the wake of an acute sense of having been emotionally swindled -- that they had been cunningly set up from the start. It is sometimes easier to accept that one has been deliberately conned rather than to believe that one's pain is merely the unintended by-product of another person's selfish indifference. (Yet, after having exhaustively studied innumerable instances of narcissistic giving, that is what I believe is the prototypical scenario: the narcissistic giver -- unless, of course, sadism is an important ingredient -- is essentially oblivious to the interpersonal let down for which his behavior is an indisputable catalyst).

Furthermore, this erroneous attribution (that the intent is malign) in applied not only to narcissistic givers, but to narcissists in general: *i.e., a paranoid sense of being persecuted is often defensively reinforced after one has*

10

suffered a narcissistic injury because it is preferable and less painful to feel plotted against than to experience oneself as having been existentially discounted.

Narcissistic giving as a pattern of defensive behavior, emblematic of a contemporary failure to be intimate or to relate, is so widespread that it cannot possibly be restricted to either the business or professional world. By my own conservative tally, it occurs millions of times daily in America in all walks of life. Although its aftermath is typically negative, often attended by a confused sense of amorphous dissatisfaction, its underlying dynamics are invariably inaccessible to both parties -- which is another way of saying that before narcissistic giving can take place there must be collusion. Of course there are other defenses against the manifold anxieties engendered by the constraints of intimacy, but narcissistic giving may be the most commonplace, global and therefore best suited metaphor. (Besides, since every defense against intimacy entails a denial of sorts that there is an underlying impairment of the ability to relate, it follows there is always a corresponding insinuation that one is offering more than one really is -- which is the sine qua non of narcissistic giving).

It is fashionable today to trace the origins of maladaptive relating: children of alcoholics, children of abusive parents, children of narcissists, children of dysfunctional families. What is often overlooked is the glaring outcome of such impediments to closeness: perhaps the paradigmatic malaise of our time -- *pathological absence of intimacy*. And toward that goal, to paint the way to a better understanding of what intimacy is, I devote the bulk of this book to its antipode: narcissistic giving. Although it is a serious study intended for experts in human relations, it is written in non-technical language in order to reach as broad an audience as possible.

In my first book, *Portrait of The Artist as a Young Patient*, I used the persona of the struggling, yet-to-be born, socially invisible artist as a symbol to draw attention to an overlooked class of displaced persons, the creative homeless. In this book I want to show that what might be called the most meaningfully creative aspect of human relating -- intimacy -- is somewhat of a lost art that contemporarily is represented by its counterfeit, narcissistic giving.

To do that I draw on material culled from my practice as a therapist and my own experience living in a world and a time that is brimful of narcissistic giving. Thus, the first chapter, *Everyday Examples*, paints a wide spectrum to denote the scope of the problem. The second chapter, *Strategies of Narcissistic Giving*, examines some of the underlying dynamic processes. The third chapter,

The Mirror Up To Nature, uses the concept of narcissistic giving as a tool with which to understand some of the ways a public starved for true nurturance pursues and receives substitutive pleasure from the entertainment industry. The fourth chapter, *Narcissistic Giving in The Mental Health Profession*, is an attempt to apply what I think I have learned to my own field.

The concluding fifth chapter, *Intimate Giving*, sketches a provisional outline of what I believe to be some of the constituents of true intimacy. If, as I contend, narcissistic giving is the antipode of authentic relating, the quintessence of what it is not, then by a method of simple *reversal*, a roughly accurate picture should come into focus of what intimacy, as manifesting in intimate giving, is.

It is the reason I wrote the book.

CHAPTER ONE

Everyday Examples

WHY NARCISSISTIC GIVING IS SUCH A UNIVERSAL DEFENSE

It simultaneously generates pleasure while furnishing a necessary defense. In other words, it is a defensive operation with a secondary gain as opposed, for example, to primary repression which protects the psyche by helping it to steer away from pain or to head off a threatening increase in anxiety. For good reason Freud considered repression the prototypical defense mechanism: indeed certain defense mechanisms (e.g. signal anxiety) owe their existence -- being both activates and positively reinforced -- to their capacity to foretell situations likely to inspire dread. In such instances, it is easy to see that the chief defensive benefit is a preventive one arising from the reduction in anticipatory tension, and ensuing feeling of relief, which are thereby brought about.

This is quite different from a second class of defensive operations which offer both pleasure and safety at the same time. In the latter category, in addition to narcissistic giving, fall what may be called addictive and sexual defenses: psychical strategies which depend on the peak experiences afforded by drugs, or the intense arousal induced by sexual indulgence, to act as a reciprocally inhibiting force against an underlying anxiety which is being covertly defended against. To the degree the defensive maneuver incorporates reciprocal inhibition, it will not have to be so preventive; anxiety can be more easily ignored, or, when it does arise -- smothered. Because of that, a defense of this kind will tend to be more slipshod, impervious to time and conducive to acting out. In this light, it may be seen that part of the reason addictive defenses are so addictive, lies in their ability to be vividly and effectively operationalized at almost any moment (in contradistinction to repression where exact timing is called for in order to bar from consciousness the emergence of something deemed to be anxiety-provoking).

A long time ago, the psychoanalyst Otto Fenichel pointed out that people may engage in sexual behavior not because they want pleasure but because they wish to avoid pain: at no time has that been more true than it is today when addictive defenses have reached almost epidemic proportions. Since strong affect can be engendered with sinister ease through sexual enactment or the ingestion of drugs, these acting out defenses -- that do not require the ego strength of old-fashioned repression which has to muster, without assistance, its own energetic counterforce -- are accessible to almost everyone (where, basically, all you have to do is ride the affective crest of an induced mood).

As a defense, narcissistic giving may or may not be addictive but it is acting out in the sense that acting out always implies interpersonal exploitation of some degree. It owes its universality as should be clear, to a number of factors: it is operationally simple and can be activated at almost any time; it generally feels good (is ego syntonic) and thereby provides immediate, secondary gain; and, as an almost added reinforcing defense, it contains an efficient form of denial -- i.e. I do not have nothing to give, I have, in fact, more than enough. Each of the everyday examples which follows is intended to illuminate an aspect of that universality and -- although countless other instances could perhaps have been as appropriately selected -- it is hoped their accumulated weight will bring into sharper relief a potent force which, although characteristically disavowed, seems to be gathering momentum in our present culture.

THE WRONG GIFT

To continue, briefly, with the story of my friend who, despite having written a brilliant book, had failed to win the interest or backing of his publisher. Following his disappointing conversation with his publicist, he had immersed himself in a personal word-of-mouth campaign to publicize his book by diligently contacting anyone he knew whom he thought might conceivably have a bearing on its distribution. Although the fruit of such enthusiastic self-promotion was not entirely negligible, it hardly offset the overall sales figures which continued to be depressingly low. By then, my friend had taken to the habit of consulting his publisher's marketing manager on the first of each month to hear firsthand (from the latest computer printout) the number of his books which had been sold for the preceding thirty days. Accordingly, half a year after he had been published, by which time a picture of his impact upon the general reading public should have been emerging, he inquired, once again, as to what the current sales figures showed. To which the marketing manager, in a lively celebratory tone, proclaimed, "We sold 108 books for October, thanks mostly to your efforts."

As in the previous example where the publicist had off-handedly offered her credentials as the antidote to his disheartenment, this simple statement condensed a world of non-giving. In addition, it illustrated with admirable clarity one of the most popular strategies for not giving: which is, to overlook the explicit or implicit request (in this instance, to address the appalling dearth of sales -- only 108 books sold nationwide for an entire month is, by any standard, shocking -- and the publisher's manifest impotence to reverse the trend and to offer any hope in the foreseeable future) and to direct itself instead, under the guise of graciously acknowledging the contribution of the author, to some, at best, obliquely related need (e.g. the natural desire to be patted on the back when one is obviously doing a good job).

Such a tactic might be called that of *tangential nurturing* wherein the intent plainly is to provide a substitute gratification which can compensate the person enough to deflect his attention away from the inherent frustration in not being heard. When narcissistic giving takes this form, there is always frustration because even if the compensatory bribe has been truly satisfying on some level, there is an unavoidable, underlying, nagging sense that one does not matter since one has not been fundamentally listened to: i.e. the so-called gift does not realistically reflect a recognition of the would-be beneficiary's need, but instead is bestowed as though it is a measure of the giver's generosity.

This is another way of saying, as this example clearly shows, that narcissistic giving is a non-intimate act and interaction par excellence in which the giving is never meaningfully connected to the receiving and is therefore properly characterized by its profound absence of empathy and attunement (the effect is often painfully analogous to that of accepting a present that one subsequently perceives was given to meet the needs and interests of the giver and not the receiver). And it may be better understood if one takes into account a salient narcissistic trait of the grandiose self -- to wit, that it believes it can relate to the other solely by consulting with its own perceptions: which is evident in the case of narcissistic giving where the gift is invariably something that initially is not wanted. In this light it can be seen that one important reason the narcissist lacks empathy is because -- believing he can dispense with it -- he finds no reason to cultivate it.

FAIL-SAFE RELATING

In order to demonstrate that the incident I have described was by no means an isolated one, I would like to compare it with an analogous experience of my own, one which moreover reveals yet another aspect of narcissistic giving. It concerns my very first nonfiction book (*Portrait of the Artist as a Young Patient*) and it goes back to a time -- shortly after its completion -- when I was especially vulnerable to the writer's paradigmatic anxiety that his work may not succeed in getting published. So I was overjoyed, as was my agent, when I unexpectedly received word that a prestigious editor from a leading publishing house had not only become interested in my book but was eager to meet me in person to discuss the prospects for publication.

Thus, I was baptized into my initial author-editor luncheon date and for about two hours basked in the pleasure of hearing a reputed authority figure not only commend what I had done, but personally declare how much she had loved reading my manuscript. When she was done, Melanie (as I'll call her) matter-of-factly mentioned that the next step was to turn my book over to something called the committee, who needed to deliver a final approval before an official offer to publish could be made. The function of the committee, she pointed out, was to make sure that the book was of interest to the general public as well as to select professionals, but she added that -- although nothing was certain -- her input as editor in chief of their distinguished professional division, would "count enormously."

So, for a delirious moment hope soared, as there seemed no way I could lose: If the committee assented, I would be broadly introduced to the public at large; if they demurred, I could rely on my advocate, Melanie, to enlist me into her own group of restricted but respected professionals -- and I quietly voiced my optimism, "In other words, even if the committee turns me down, you'll accept me as one of your professional books."

After what had seemed hours of uninterrupted social pleasantry, a chill descended as Melanie, turning strangely mercenary, dryly informed me, "This is definitely a book for the general public. These days you have to be very clear in what your marketing concept is. And I don't think your agent would be happy to get less money."

It dawned on me, although I could not put my finger on the origin of my revelation at the time, that something was wrong. On the one hand, Melanie was ostensibly championing my interests (and my agent's), sagely advising me that the best way to maximize my profits was to home in on the potentially strongest available market. On the other hand, by passing up the option she apparently had to ensure my publication -- by including me under her own auspices -- she was deliberately settling for a curiously passive, spectator's role in the decision-making process that was going to determine the ultimate publication fate of the book she professed to love.

Three weeks later, when the committee unanimously declined to publish me, when it had become clear to me that Melanie had never had any intention of going out on a limb and backing the book which she had repeatedly called "wonderful", I was able to at least salvage from a very disheartening experience an important insight into the process of narcissistic giving.

And what I had then understood better than before was the connection between narcissistic giving and what may be called *fail-safe relating*: i.e. the endeavor -- by making sure that one takes as little risk as possible -- to derive only benefits from interpersonal interactions. While it is easy to see, when put in these terms, that this is impossible, what is remarkable is how frequently people will attempt with the straightest of faces to pull this off. Part of the attraction must be that since nothing is going to be invested, nothing can be lost. Thus, in the worst case scenario in which none of the hoped-for benefits are forthcoming, there is always the consolation that one has only gambled on a no-lose interpersonal bet.

In this light, narcissistic giving is a nearly perfect example of fail-safe relating, and since it is based on denial, there is the spurious promise that -- far from bothering to protect one's legitimate needs -- one is instead altruistically focused on safeguarding the rights of the other (e.g. Melanie's "I don't think your agent would be happy to get less money.")

It is characteristic of narcissistic giving that such postures of altruism are thoroughly bogus: in the example of Melanie, real giving -- as opposed to the pretense of watching out for both the interests of myself and my agent -- would have been to have personally assumed the responsibility and risk for either publishing or not publishing my book and to have at some point directly communicated her honest intentions one way or the other.

By adopting this altruistic attitude, narcissistic giving circumvents the underlying existential guilt that -- since one is putting nothing of oneself into one's actions -- one cannot legitimately assume responsibility for them and therefore cannot authentically own them. It thereby seemingly takes for granted that one is responsible for one's behavior and can therefore afford to focus on the higher, more selfless aim of inculcating in the other an awareness of how to be truly sensitive to his or her neglected needs.

Thus, with hindsight, I was able to understand that Melanie, despite her unrelenting protestations of appreciation and commitment to my book, had chosen to take no personal risk, whatsoever, and to instead totally defer all involvement to an impersonal committee while simultaneously trying to hang onto and cash in on any possible future benefits by maintaining an attitude and promise of support. One of the pernicious side effects of this kind of fail-safe narcissitic giving, as I can personally testify, is that it does not acknowledge its intention of giving nothing (which at the very least would helpfully define boundaries by realistically lowering expectations) but aspires through spurious over-promising to have its cake and eat it too: i.e. to avoid risk, while obtaining benefits.

It is one measure of the profound disheartenment which people today feel when it comes to receiving basic nurturance from a prospective partner that, far more than the reverse, they will accept a decidedly one-sided contract: that is, they will stick around in an ongoing relationship that offers at best emotional crumbs on the scant chance that the tantalizing promises of narcissistic giving may one day be fulfilled.

NARCISSISTIC STRENGTH
(or, I love my Achilles Heel)

The denial intrinsic to narcissistic giving, without which defensive operations such as tangential nurturing and fail-safe relating could not be carried out, perhaps reaches its pinnacle in something (which for want of a better name) I have called *narcissistic strength*. Simply put, what this means is that there is probably no more effective way to deny that one has a weakness than to single it out as a strength -- as though to say that one is not only not embarrassed and has nothing to apologize for, but is in fact quite proud of the alleged deficit. Thus, someone who, for example, is often perceived as combative and mean-spirited may be fond of proclaiming, "I'm not a nice guy," or, "Nice guys finish last"; or someone known to hold grudges upon perceiving himself the target of a clear-cut injustice, may cheerfully corroborate this with, "I don't get mad, I get even"; or someone who plainly enjoys the spectacle of another person squirming in embarrassment may volunteer, "I guess I'm a sadist;" or someone, habitually demonstrating little interest in the needs or feelings of others, may boast, "I look out for number one," or "Charity begins at home."

Once again what is amazing is how relatively successful these crude maneuvers are. Of all the instances when I have either directly observed it or heard about it secondhand, I cannot recall even a single time when anyone chose to confront the none-too-subtle issue: i.e. as, for example -- to the person who admits to being comfortable with the identity of sadist -- to bluntly inquire, "Why should you want to be a sadist?"

In the case of the latter, part of the reason is intimidation: there is something more than a little bit frightening about someone who genuinely appears at ease with being what others would consider disturbingly antisocial. To the degree that such a person palpably derives satisfaction from grossly antisocial behavior, there can arise a suspicion of psychopathic potential (or, what has been psychologically termed pathological narcissistic aggression) and there will be an understandable tendency to collude through silence, so as not to provoke the person to feel obliged to have to prove what he says at your expense.

Generally speaking, narcissistic giving -- which at least goes through the motions of addressing the needs of the other -- is less threatening than a display of narcissistic strength, where there is no longer any pretense of caring about anyone else. (It should be noted that narcissistic strength is often reinforced by its own brand of implicit denial -- *narcissistic honesty*: i.e. the grandiose belief that if one brazenly and publicly admits one's most glaring shortcomings (e.g. "I know I have a terrible temper") one is somehow thereby exonerated from the responsibility of remedying them).

There are thus no fine lines but instead a series of gradations between narcissistic giving (which specializes in placating but not satisfying), narcissism proper where there is an obvious absorption with the needs of the self, and so-called narcissistic strength which flaunts its antisocial character traits in the other's face.

RELATING THROUGH THE DISPENSING OF
INFORMATION AND INSTRUCTION

Few things could rattle Max, my patient, as thoroughly as a brief telephone call from his older sister who lived over a thousand miles away and whom he had seen less than a handful of times during the past ten years. In an effort to understand why, he would repeat verbatim in the session the latest message from his sister (which on average lasted about fifteen seconds). A typical message might run:

"It's Dad's fiftieth wedding anniversary, and Mother's birthday next Tuesday. A card from you would be appreciated. If you want to call, Dad's home from the hospital. He'd love to hear from you. Hope you're well."

From having worked with Max for several years, in the course of which I had had literally dozens of such staccato salutations directed to his answering machine faithfully reported back to me, I was able to insert such abbreviated exchanges into the meaningful context of a lifelong relationship. And it had become increasingly clear that Max still resented his sister's insistence on communicating from the authoritarian stance (which he had been aware of from earliest childhood); that he became fixated on whatever she said which he could construe as bossy or intrusive (which included nearly everything); and that once so preoccupied it became impossible for him to relate in anything but a defensively insecure and hostile fashion.

For my own part, and from the standpoint of my ongoing interest in examples of narcissistic giving, I could not help but be struck by how each of his sister's utterances, no matter how terse -- under the guise of merely imparting inside family news or dispensing helpful instruction -- was in actuality a masterpiece of non-giving which managed to effectively ignore a number of Max's well-articulated needs. To wit, that he hated being off-handedly reminded of what his family obligations were, especially by his sister; that, as a matter of fact, he (in contrast to his sister) had long made a habit of *not* sending birthday and wedding anniversary cards which he regarded as ritualized sentimentality; and that he positively bristled whenever he was instructed in any way, the more so if the instruction were unsolicited.

As Max had ironically noted, after exhausting his list of gripes against this short but deadly message, the one thing he really would have been interested in knowing -- the up-to-date condition of his father's health, and what the doctor had had to say about his recent stay in the hospital -- his sister had for some reason elected to withhold.

This is not the place to go into the etiology and dynamics of the evident animosity which existed between Max and his sister. Instead, I would like to emphasize one important defensive manifestation of that underlying animosity which, as shown in the example of his sister's telephone message, was to provide almost entirely useless information. There are few better strategies for seemingly giving without having to bother to relate, than to give information. Since we live in a time of information-overload and in a society which is fearful of missing out on the possibility of relevant data, one can never be too sure that a given piece of information, regardless of how trivial-sounding, may not have some present or future usefulness; and therefore one can never be too certain that one is not being given something when -- in response to an explicit or implicit emotional need -- even neutral information is relayed.

For that reason alone, an interpersonal response which is essentially informational is often surprisingly successful in diverting attention away from the intrinsic poverty of true emotional sustenance or nurturing intention. When the information being purveyed is factually, logically or superficially connected to the specific need being raised, it can seem almost seductively relevant. What's more, since someone in need is often covertly or directly searching for "an answer," the confident air of crisply dispensing precise information can imperceptibly and wishfully be elevated into the reassuring proficiency of the expert, someone with just the right know-how that is needed to remedy the situation. Again, what is almost invariably overlooked in such a transaction, is that nothing is easier to do (than to distribute facts) and nothing is further from intimacy. While this is not intended to deny a place of importance for pertinent and helpful information in specialized circumstances, it is to say that it is a sad commentary on the state of contemporary relatedness, that what in fact are essentially informational crumbs, are often embraced as satisfying instances of giving.

Relating through the dispensing of instruction is perhaps an even more cogent example of narcissistic giving, inasmuch as an instruction typically carries the stamp of authority -- thereby putting the recipient on the defensive and making it deceptively difficult to explore, let alone challenge, the ulterior motive of the interaction. The metamessage of an instruction is that the one who instructs is in a one-up position, entitling the person to be at least a provisional caretaker. In addition, by showing sufficient concern to assume the responsibility for briefly taking over, it can seem that one is doing something far more urgent than merely being empathic: one is actually attempting to *resolve* the situation. And, on a deeper level, there is the secondary gain that unconscious anxiety over how to cope with the real relationship can be displaced onto the palpable control issues usually stirred up by the superior stance of instructor. In other words, anxiety over the threat of being or not being intimate with another person, can be successfully discharged into absorbing mini-battles over whether one wants, or does not want, to be told what to do.

It seems to be true and is important that often to the degree someone feels unequipped to be close with another person there will be a reliance on and overestimation of the value of facts. To the person impaired in the capacity to give, a fact may be seen as having at least the dignity of an indisputable concrete thing, and an instruction as an assertive plan for behavioral resolution. What's more, endeavoring to provide useful information and instruction can be nostalgically evocative of parental guidance received as a child: when being informed about the ways of the world, and how to proceed in it, was a necessary act of love. Often forgotten, of course, is that in adult relationships the reverse is true -- the greater mutuality of nurturance there is, the less need to reduce matters to a question of rules, stipulations, and the enforcing of transgressions. It is the mark of a shallow relationship (and of shallow parenting) when the brunt of the interpersonal energy goes into a repetitive instructional definition of the rules or boundaries, as opposed to a nurturing exploration of the potentiality for growth.

NARCISSISTIC INTEREST
(or "Don't Call Me, I'll Call You")

Molly, a brilliant young painter, who had been seeing me as a patient for several years, had finally gathered her courage and submitted a portfolio of her slides to a curator of a local art gallery -- in the hope of attaining a first showing of her work. Having worked with a number of such aspiring artists, and knowing from firsthand experience how trying the wait can be for the first public recognition of one's professional worth, I was naturally eager to learn what kind of reception lay in store for her. When several months passed by without a word of feedback, and it became clear that Molly -- becoming increasingly convinced of the inevitability of rejection -- was suffering terribly and unnecessarily under the weight of unrelieved suspense, I finally ventured to point out that there was nothing preventing her from inquiring as to the status of her portfolio review. Thus bolstered, she screwed up her courage a second time and tremulously telephoned the curator, who initially had some evident difficulty in recollecting someone called Molly. When she reminded him, as pleasantly, lightly and firmly as she could, that some months ago she had submitted her portfolio of slides to his custody and had received in return a promise to survey them -- the curator professed to remember. After a brief pause, during which it seemed to Molly that he was mentally tracking down her portfolio (that perhaps was only one among hundreds) he announced, "I'm skimming it now."

Which, not surprisingly, both baffled and disheartened Molly, who in the session immediately following her long-awaited contact with the curator, repeatedly wondered aloud what it was that she had at last learned? She had been told, on the one hand, with quiet but unmistakable authority, that he was presently "skimming it" as though there were something portentous in that, or at least portentous enough to stand as a reasonable response to her obviously meaning-laden inquiry. Yet, on the other hand, the prosaic, laconic tone with which she had been answered, strongly suggested the curator thought the question less than substantive, a matter that could be dispensed with speedily and routinely.

As with my colleague, who had been politely but regularly discounted by his publisher, I could not refrain from drawing Molly's attention to just how remarkably non-giving the curator, in just four words, had managed to be. In retrospect, it seemed that almost any simple honest statement, such as, "I'm just beginning to look at it," or, "I've looked at about four slides so far, and here's what I think . . .", would have been in the long run considerably more helpful to Molly because -- regardless of how appreciative or critical of her work the curator may in fact have been -- she would have been afforded the opportunity of at least confronting the reality of her situation.

I mention this example because it illustrates another important characteristic of narcissistic giving which, again, for lack of a better name, might be called *narcissistic interest*. By that I mean the characterological tendency of certain people to regard the interests of others as essentially possibilities for exploitation in the overriding goal of gratifying their particular aims; and nothing shows this more clearly than the fact that, when objectively looked at side by side, there is typically almost no connection between the professed interest of the parties who are presumably mutually and beneficially interacting. Thus, in the case of Molly, there was no conjunction between her own unmistakable deep-seated interest in securing a first official recognition of the professional worth of her work, and the perhaps reciprocally inverse desire of the beleaguered curator not to get mired in the sticky role of being the one who either answers or spurns the prayers of young artists, yet somehow does not lose face while shirking his responsibility.

It is the genius of narcissistic giving that such glaring incongruity of needs is generally obfuscated by its insistence that not only is there a common ground, but that it is strong enough and exciting enough to inspire a spontaneous investment of interest and energy in the other. And, as already mentioned, it is exceedingly difficult to challenge this strategy without appearing, to an embarrassing degree, to be either ungrateful or greedy.

As a consequence of this privileged position of rarely being confronted, someone acting to implement narcissistic interest will predictably misconstrue the real aims of the other (although pretending otherwise) while continuing to be grandiose enough to believe that such displays of pseudo involvement and shallow or pretentious giving will magically be sufficient to meet the other's genuine needs. And this is borne out in the frequent observation that when given the slightest encouragement -- if, for example, the would-be beneficiary colludes by appearing to accept the putative gift -- the narcissistic giver typically experiences an upsurge of what could be called false-self self esteem.

When there is an inequity of power between the narcissistic giver and the aspiring beneficiary -- as there often is and as was the case with Molly in her pursuit of a favorable review from the all-powerful curator -- the underlying agenda of the empowered narcissistic giver (i.e., preponderant self-interest) can rise more freely to the surface in the sometimes candid admission of a need to exercise one-way control. Thus, understandably uncertain as to the portent of the curator's pithy, but meaningless, "I'm skimming it now," Molly had mildly inquired whether she might contact him at some future point in the hope of obtaining at least a more conclusive commentary and was told: "Don't call me, I'll call you."

It is easy to see, in terms of our discussion of narcissistic-giving interest, that what this answer, or stipulation really means, is: "The only contact I wish with you, is not when you or even we should feel the need for it, but when *I* want it." In other words, contact or interaction is to be implemented and arranged strictly on the basis of only one person's initiative. It is for that reason, the phrase -- stereotypical, lampooned and even famous -- contains much of the essence of non-intimacy: the profound absence of mutuality and resonance with the other's needs; an interpersonal set up in which a single person unfortunately has the power to preempt the timing of the contact, the conditions of the contact and the purpose of the contact.

FOCUSING ON THE OTHER PERSON'S FEELINGS
(or "I'm Only Thinking of You")

Charles, another of my patients, although extremely intelligent, sensitive, and gifted when it came to perceiving, empathizing with, and nurturing the feelings of others, was seemingly incapable of doing the same for himself. That is to say he typically felt left out in the cold when -- after an interesting, tense, or meaningful encounter with another person -- it came time to sort out and determine what it was he had just experienced. Although often prescient and precise in regard to the nuances of someone else's shifting emotions, he could be confoundingly obtuse, detached and unreceptive to his own inner states. Over the course of time, and over many sessions, it became clear to Charles (and to me) that such ignorance of the self was neither accidental nor unmediated: that is, there was a defensive need, and therefore payoff, to be always more or less extremely and unilaterally attuned.

In the case of Charles, and many others like him, the defensive payoff lay in the measure of control afforded by the interpersonal pose of altruistically skipping over one's personal reactions, tensions, anxieties or conflicts and focusing instead on the other person's feelings. The implication then is that this is what is really important, what needs to be addressed and tended to. Which in turn subtly suggests that the emotional equilibrium of the other must be sufficiently out of order if it is attracting the attention of an outside observer (who, by inference, must be by comparison, emotionally together at least during the time he is able to concentrate on the apparent distress of another person).

When such is not the case (as it was not with Charles) when the so-called impartial outside observer -- far from being just an empathic good samaritan offering the much-needed services of therapeutic confidant -- is actually himself affectively embroiled in the interaction at hand but is opting to deny this with the altruistic banner of narcissistic giving, then it is necessary to look for a hidden agenda. And the time when it will be most evident will probably occur when the self-appointed objective observer happens to be under particular stress: so that the palpable strain of laboring to preserve an unreal interpersonal stance of uninterrupted altruistic interest will sooner or later betray the disavowed narcissism.

What is then revealed is that the person -- unable in the first place to deal candidly, reciprocally and intimately with someone else -- will, especially under duress, attempt to restore control by taking flight from his own emotions through the principal strategy of making the other's feelings the entire designated sphere of interaction.

Typically, when this gets transacted, the other feels stifled, somehow "bested" or controlled. Almost never does the other feel given to and this is so especially when the person suspects that somehow he or she is being subjected to a cunning display of mental health one-upmanship by someone who, on a disavowed level, may be just as angry, anxious or upset as he or she is, but is refusing to admit it. (There is then resentment, voiced in the frequent complaint that the person who is presuming to be only altruistically inclined, is covertly being "moralistic.")

Because of this, the strategy of relating through making the other person's feelings the primary set of responses to be reacted to, works best when the narcissistic giver in the scenario is not unduly, visibly affected and can concentrate with convincing equanimity on the task of appearing empathic. And, in point of fact, such people, through long practice, are generally rather expert at soothing and quieting in others the routine disappointments and inevitable agitations of ordinary life. What then goes unnoticed, is that to attempt to relate as a kind of lay counselor, someone who can be counted on to react non-directly, neutrally and objectively -- when you are *not* a counselor -- is equivalent in everyday life to not relating as a person.

"THIS and THAT"

Jane, a patient, was inordinately sensitive to slights, especially slights delivered by those whom she regarded as insignificant others in her life, meaning those with whom she had a purely social relationship. It was bad enough to feel cheated in relationships that originally had seemed promising, but, somehow, for a chance acquaintance or near total stranger to subtly put her down -- under the guise of making innocent small talk or just being neighborly -- was more than she could bear. She therefore regularly examined such interactions for innuendos of devaluation, and when she found them (which, not surprisingly, was quite often) she would bring them into therapy to discuss, and to ruminate upon their impact.

While I recognized that Jane was finely attuned to, and even actively searched for instances of disavowed, social rebuff, I could not help but be struck by her unerring ability to ferret out from under the smoke screen of conversational banality profound impairments in the capacity to relate. Thus, the colloquial phrase "this and that" could evoke her ire, especially when it was used as a convenient generality with which to dodge a specific relevant question or to gloss over an uncomfortable personal experience. Perhaps no one symbolized the art of making conversation, while managing to say nothing at all as much as a certain neighbor -- a man she ruefully dubbed "The Plant Man" because of his fondness for sitting nearly motionless on his outside stoop, day in and day out, and restricting his communication not only with her but with everyone, to the barest remarks on the current weather, violations of parking regulations he had chronicled, or oddities in the street he had witnessed.

More than any other patient, Jane sharpened my awareness of how conversational mores, verbal clichés, or so-called social amenities could be used not only as shields to cover glaring relational deficits, but could stand as symbols in themselves of such impairment (and were easy to see once one became accustomed to regarding them from the standpoint of narcissistic giving).

And from that perspective, the homely phrase "this and that" -- purporting to be an answer or statement cast as a congenial, colloquialism, as though to say, "well, one thing or another" -- can reveal a world of meaning: its narcissistic-giving component being particularly evident at just those times when someone is expressing a clear non-trivial need for something personal and specific. By seemingly offering to describe something singular and perhaps rich ("this and that"), and almost instantaneously stopping short without having delivered anything, the person using this phrase can succeed in both stimulating and frustrating his audience; and by typically hurrying on in a feigned nonchalant manner (as though something has just been thereby clarified) to the next conversational point, the auditor can be left with a peculiar empty-handed feeling, the emotional equivalent to the tennis version of being "wrong-footed."

Of course, the phrase "this and that" is only one of a catalogue or family of conversational generalities regularly employed to help fill the void of non-relating. Probably the most famous example of this is the practice and belief that by empathically reporting on the weather, a connection can somehow be made: Jane's abiding aversion to her neighbor whose entire conversational style was pinned to the superficies of daily life, is but an extreme instance of the kind of paranoia that can develop when a sensitive person begins to suspect that he or she is being spoken to, and interacted with, in an essentially non-communicative fashion. When this is a pattern, as it is in many contemporary relationships, the narcissistic injury that one normally feels upon being narcissistically given to, can grow into a paranoid vigilance (as it did in Jane) in which everything the other says or does is scrutinized in order to determine why it is so necessary to keep the real self perpetually hidden beneath banalities.

While it is commonplace to denigrate instances of non-conversation, such as talking about the weather, as superficial what is overlooked is how often what it conceals is a grave absence of the ability to relate. This may not always have been the case. It may be that an ethologist of the stamp of Konrad Lorenz (who was interested in tracing existing cultural and social rituals back to their putative, pre-human, biological origins) could persuasively argue that before the dawn of civilization there was a time when the weather -- in its capacity to either favor or threaten basic survival -- really mattered; and that talking about the weather meant talking about a life-or-death issue. Yet, even if that were the origin of relating through commentary on the ecosystem, in today's world of a technologically monitored environment, nothing could be of less personal significance and therefore further removed from intimacy.

In spite of this, and to an extraordinary degree, there are many relationships which are founded on interactions designed to avoid intimacy and to deny that one is avoiding intimacy by pretending (narcissistic giving) that one is somehow, if only momentarily, connecting with another person. And seen this way, many conversational social mores -- such as being obliged to verbally acknowledge that one is glad to meet, and glad to have met every new person one has ever been introduced to -- have the function of repudiating in the course of mundane or random interpersonal interactions an often persistent and disquieting premonition: we are strangers who have nothing to offer one another.

"I'LL DRINK TO THAT"

To return to Molly. Shortly after she had submitted her portfolio of slides to the curator of a local art gallery she decided to pay a visit to her parents who lived in Denver and whom she had not seen for several years. Emboldened by her decision to achieve a first showing of her work, she resolved to take the even bigger risk of allowing her parents to not only inspect, but to personally own a series of watercolors she had recently completed, and was subsequently overjoyed at their seemingly unabashed pride. Her father, in particular, who insisted on showing them to everyone and anyone: his boss at the insurance firm; his mechanic at the garage; his nephew in grammar school; the doorman to his building -- and then hurrying back to his daughter with reports of their praise.

After a week of such eulogizing, it dawned on Molly that she had not once observed either of her parents actually look at a single watercolor. And not once had she heard either of them say anything -- outside of recounting the opinions of others -- about the painting themselves. So, on the eve of her departure, once more screwing up her courage, she surprised her father by suddenly asking him why it was she had yet to see him look at the pictures or hear him personally comment on them. To which, she was flatly told, "Painting is over my head."

The moral of this true story is simply that the reader should beware of what might be called the tactic of the false celebration: that is, looking for a superficial or peripheral reason to get excited -- e.g., the alcoholic who searches for a social occasion to celebrate as a justification for feeding his addiction (thus "I'll drink to that") -- so as to defer having to do the painstaking, sober work of relating. When that occurs, the narcissistic-giving component lies in acting as though the cause of the celebration is the wish to honor the accomplishment or good fortune of another, instead of (which is the case) the desire to find a face-saving but entertaining smoke screen for one's inability to take someone else seriously. Perhaps even more subversive, is that typically the narcissistic giver not only initiates, but orchestrates, the pseudo celebration -- making it that much more difficult to challenge the authenticity of the presumed gift.

And in this light, the fact that it took Molly an entire week to ask her father the most obvious of questions and the only question that mattered (whether *he* had looked at the paintings) becomes understandable.

WAITING FOR GODOT

One of the complaints of patients who complain about their relationships, concerns what is often perceived as the "withholding" tendencies of their partners. Rather than delve into its etiology, I would like to focus on the subjective experience of someone interacting with a withholding personality and see if the concept of narcissistic giving can help make sense of what is often regarded as a baffling encounter.

And from the standpoint of narcissistic giving much of what the withholding personality does, makes sense. Thus, the withholding personality characteristically achieves much of its aggravating impact through stalling and, so to speak, emotionally buying time. Interpersonally, the message seems to be that the timing and circumstances are all wrong for a relationship properly to begin. What is less apparent, is that the person who withholds is simultaneously deflecting attention away -- by displacing the supposed deficiency or communicational snafu onto the other -- from the very real possibility that he may be the one responsible for the delay. It therefore follows that a favorite tactic of the withholding person is to echo or paraphrase whatever has been directed at him in an ironic, disparaging tone: e.g. "Do I *like* going to the movies?"; "How do I *feel* about working with you?" "I remind you of someone you used to know?"

The implication, in effect, is that there is something wrong, odd, out of synch, unclear or at any rate inappropriate in the other's overture or request for communication, and the other is therefore merely being asked to redefine or better define the purpose of the inquiry before it can be taken seriously enough to justify the energetic expenditure, howsoever minimal, of an initial straightforward response. As for his part, the withholding person seems to be saying that he is not interested in wasting his time and that so far he has not seen a good enough reason for investing in a reply.

Now at this point, an unfortunate dynamic gets set up. Since it is understandably painful to be brushed off before one can even begin to make one's point, there is a tendency to deny that this is really what has happened and to assume instead that only a misunderstanding has arisen. And thereby the other falls into the well-laid trap of shouldering the burden of blame for the false start, by trying to restart in an improved fashion. Not surprisingly, the scenario is repeated: the withholding person continues to be unimpressed and distinctly uninterested in whatever the other seems to want, while the other, depending on the quota of available self-esteem, can range from being justifiably angry, discouraged, self-critical, withholding in turn or resentful of a perceived rejection.

Such unconsciously premeditated diffidence on the part of someone who wishes to withhold can, of course, assume many forms. One of the most popular is, at a certain juncture, to appear to respond to the request for an interaction of some kind -- but to do so with an air of resignation, in which case the other is often left so unsatisfied as to regret having gone to the trouble in the first place (exactly the aftermath desired by the withholding person).

The following scenario involving someone who initiates and someone who withholds is a common one, variations of which, I have heard from numerous patients:

"Do you ever listen to talk radio?"

"Do I ever *listen* to talk radio?"

"Oh, yes. There are few things I really enjoy as much as listening to a good guest on a talk radio program."

"Talk radio is not one of the things I enjoy."

By tactics such as these, the person who withholds makes it clear that whatever relational possibilities exist can only be actualized in the future, presumably after the other has gotten his or her act together so as to be worthy of the hypothetical encounter. In stark contrast to most instances of narcissistic giving wherein the necessary component of spurious over-promise is immediately and tantalizingly put up front, it is here pointedly both dangled and deferred. This is because in the case of the withholding personality the component of over-promise hinges on the claim that at some optimal time in the future, the relational goods which are presumed to be present may be delivered. It is a spurious over-promise since there is no reason whatsoever to believe that the person who is presently withholding is going to be any less so in the nearby future. Unless, of course, there is evidence that he is undergoing a dynamic, structural change that will have the effect of transforming him into a giving, forthcoming and spontaneously nurturing person. Waiting for that to happen, however, is, as one exasperated patient once put it to me "like waiting for Godot."

It should be noted that the dynamics of the withholding person are somewhat similar to those of the person who elects to focus primarily on the feelings of the other inasmuch as both play a waiting, reactive game; and are comparable to the strategy of fail-safe relating, inasmuch as both aspire to get something for nothing.

Thus, the person who withholds is preeminently and subversively indirect while refusing to take chances. In order to do this, distance is required and this is created by two maneuvers and from two ends: on the one hand, the person pulls back from his side so as to be safely out of reach (i.e. by withholding) and .on the other hand endeavors to drive back someone, perceived as an annoying solicitor, through the tactics of repeated, covert demoralization and rejection.

By an ironic twist, the narcissistic-giving component arises from an ambivalence when it actually comes down to letting go of the proffered relationship. For such a person not only withholds, but holds on, and in order to hold on it is necessary to make some kind of grandiose promise so as to compensate for the undeniable frustration intrinsic to his basic style of relating. The reason he holds on is that in order to withhold you need someone to withhold *from*. Or to put it another way, the person who characterologically withholds, on some level seeks the satisfaction to be gained from the experience of frustrating the needs of another, and this cannot be done without a colluding partner.

Seen in this light, narcissistic giving provides a ready made and beautiful mechanism by which to accomplish these aims.

CALLING THE BLUFF OF THE NARCISSISTIC GIVER

Once someone decides for whatever reason (e.g. awareness gained through the process of psychotherapy) to no longer settle for narcissistic giving and to instead actively seek something more substantial and nourishing -- relationships that have lasted for years can seemingly almost magically dissolve. What this shows, perhaps more clearly than anything else, is the fragility of a relationship which is based on narcissistic giving. Such fragility -- reinforced by a persistent sense that there is nothing of true value to be given or received -- understandably needs to be protected by both parties, so as not to be exposed, and it therefore follows that a relationship which could be characterized as one of narcissistic giving, must be preoccupied with defensiveness and denial. That is to say, since each person sooner or later unconsciously recognizes that no genuine relating will occur, expectations are lowered and energy is diverted into salvaging whatever relational crumbs one can from an affiliation which cannot fail to disappoint. (In other words, each party grows blatantly self-absorbed as he or she painfully learns to expect less and less from the other.)

Should one of the partners, however, break the longstanding contract of silent acceptance of collusive non-giving by asking for more, it immediately becomes apparent that the narcissistic giver was all along bluffing, and that there never was any intention or capacity to deliver on the promises that were repeatedly, and seductively made. It is painful to discover this and the effect can be as though one had been building on a house of cards. When a relationship founded on narcissistic giving, that is on the unreal, is confronted with an infusion of the real (e.g., a realistic demand for a dosage of authentic intimacy), there is typically no experiential repertory of giving responses from which to draw -- and it is almost forced to dissolve.

Two people then awake to the sad realization that they have been collusively sharing an intricate self-deception. The narcissistic giver now becomes the narcissistically injured, feeling that what has been more than good enough for years is suddenly being judged defective, which can only mean that the gratitude previously expressed could not have been genuine. While the person playing the part of the supposed beneficiary, who now knows he has been settling for mere crumbs, usually angrily concludes that he has, to a humiliating degree, been duped into compromising himself.

Both sets of feelings, although coming from different circumstances, are similar in that they are almost unbearably painful. And it may be that one of the reasons the collusive denial which serves as the glue in a relationship based on narcissistic giving is characteristically so strong, is that both partners unconsciously recognize that even a single sturdy confrontation of the true nature of their pact has the power to cause a traumatic and swift demise.

THE PARANOID NARCISSISTIC GIVER

At the core of the defense of narcissistic giving lurks the fear of being exposed. Excessive reliance on narcissistic giving (when there is a chronic lack of self-esteem and deficiency of what is called ego strength) can therefore lead to a dread of being publicly shamed, which in turn can produce over time a paranoid style of relating. This is because, when a strategy of habitually promising more than one can possibly deliver is carried to an extreme, it can begin to subjectively feel that one is behaving like a con artist: i.e., all energy seems to be going into deceiving the other into believing that something of value is about to be exchanged. When the narcissistic giver does not have the antisocial or sociopathic character disorder usually associated with the professional con artist -- which can actually make such dubious emotional slight of hand an ego-syntonic, pleasurable activity -- there is an inevitable conflict between the ego and superego (conscience/ego-ideal).

Sooner or later, there is the fear that the pretending aspect of the relationship will become too obtrusive to ignore even by someone who is invested in denying the real nature of the interaction and that then, instead of being admired as one who is spontaneously bountiful, one will be exposed as a relational pauper deserving of his or her comeuppance. And at this point there may unconsciously evolve the paranoid strategy of the preemptive attack: i.e., the philosophy that offense is the best defense, which, given the initial premises, makes compelling sense.

Admittedly, the paranoid narcissistic giver being depicted is an extreme development, but it is not uncommon. Such a person typically is someone who: fragile to begin with, has the repeated sense of having spent enormous time and energy trying to placate and gratify others by any means possible (especially narcissistic giving) without receiving a trace of the hoped-for adulation; and has become unconsciously convinced that no matter what one does, one will never be respected; that instead of potential admirers to look forward to there are only detractors lying in wait and that therefore it is better to take first, before one is taken from.

As mentioned before, the other side of the coin of narcissistic giving is narcissistic injury and narcissistic injury, when it becomes generalized into a self-fulfilling prophecy, is almost indistinguishable from paranoia. To illustrate this I would like to quote verbatim a telephone conversation related to me by Ann, a patient, in which she responds to a call from her sister, Mary, who left a message expressing her concern for their aging father's mental deterioration.

  A: "Did you want to speak with me?"
  M: "I never hear from you."

A: "How's Dad?"

M: "The same. There's no point in discussing it."

A: "I spoke to him the other day and he seemed as coherent as ever."

M: "Oh, his mind is clear as a bell."

A: "So, then, he's not deteriorating mentally."

M: "He needs an eye operation."

The demoralization of the paranoid narcissistic giver (in this case, Mary) has been too great to believe in the possibility of receiving psychic nutriment and although, occasionally, as a last ditch effort, she will resort to emotional bribery, she much prefers to achieve her aims through demanding and bullying. Thus, Mary, as the example shows, who does not expect to be ever given anything by anyone including her sister, ignores Ann's invitation to talk to her and instead begins with an accusation ("I never hear from you.") Ann, who has never known how to deal with this, colludes by compliantly overlooking the devaluing implications of her sister's remark, and searches for the common ground of supposed mutual concern for the mental heath of their aging father. To which Mary responds by stepping up her attack and flatly refusing to discuss the very issue which she herself raised with an alarmist telephone message.

And, not surprisingly, Ann is provoked into assertively standing her ground by calmly pointing to her recent conversation with her father and her impression (totally contradicting that of her sister) of his continued mental competence. Not to be one-upped, Mary irrationally reverses herself ("Oh, his mind is clear as a bell."), and proclaims that the really urgent matter is that their father needs, in her opinion, an eye operation.

Thus, the paranoid narcissistic giver (as shown by Mary) seems, in many key respects, closer to the paranoid style of relating (the cognitive and characterological aspects of which have been so brilliantly delineated by David Shapiro) than to the kind of narcissistic giving that we have been attempting to portray. Through the tactic of being persistently oppositional, such a person manages to not only distance herself from but to dismiss the needs of the other. At times the disjunction can be so great, that it seems as if the paranoid person is relating entirely to her own needs and almost insisting -- as though impatient to waste time by having to actually articulate blatantly obvious thoughts -- that her mind be read: e.g., Mary stating her conviction that their father needs an eye operation without seeing the necessity for revealing a single pertinent fact leading up to her decision.

It is interesting to compare the difference between the paranoid style of relating and the strategy of conventional narcissistic giving. First, and perhaps most obvious, is the component of aggressive accusing: almost 180° opposite to the seduction-first technique of the narcissistic giver, the tactic here is the preemptive strike, which, from an interpersonal, psychological standpoint, means that a state of projected enmity, approximating pathological strife, has been intrapsychically reached.

In other words, the rationale unconsciously reinforcing the behavior of the paranoid, is that the only hope of coming away from an imminent interaction with his or her shaky world intact and not further depleted, is by an offensive thrust which successfully nips in the bud any further invasive machinations. This kind of hope is the restricted one of efficient damage control and holds no prospects for receiving positive nurturance. It follows that such a belief system will be the product of an advanced state of hopelessness when it comes to the possibility of being intimate and trusting with another person. And, superficially, this is again antithetical to the at least false hope of the narcissistic giver who presumes to initiate relationships with the expectation that by seductively flattering, gratifying and beguiling the other, he or she will be able to procure substantive narcissistic supplies. One manifest contrast, therefore, between the two styles of relating is that the narcissistic giver expects to get something (usually admiration) while the paranoid person seems to be fighting not to *lose* something (i.e., by being psychically robbed of it). In a sense, the paranoid person (let us say a woman, like Mary) relates by warning the other that she has no intention of being cheated out of whatever is rightfully hers; that she is prepared to defend her interpersonal and intrapsychic turf, if she has to; that she is very much on to the covertly acquisitive aims of the other and is capable of driving back, warding off and thwarting any suspiciously intrusive tendencies that emerge. And since such a person at this point in her development can scarcely believe in the possibility of establishing intimate rapport with another, (in fact, is threatened by it), she has little to lose by fostering with her posture of ever-ready aggressive defense an inevitably hostile climate of mutual mistrust.

In spite of these undeniable differences between the two styles of relating, they can not only co-exist, although not of course in equal measure, in the same person (as they did in Mary) but can be joined by a deep link. The deep link which underlies each style is the sense of deprivation, the feeling that one does not have any real sustenance or nurturance to give and that therefore -- when the issue is intimacy -- a way will have to be found to bypass it. The narcissistic giver does this by denial, hyperbolic seductiveness and interpersonal sleight of hand. The person who is paranoid achieves this through provocative (and therefore diverting) hostile defensiveness. The common element is that each style successfully nips in the bud the possibility of intimacy by resorting to a familiar tactic of emotional manipulation: the narcissistic giver, who relies on gratuitous flattery and the promise of instant gratification; and the embattled paranoid who hopes her series of preemptive strikes against a present opponent may wrest -- at some future time after demonstrating she can defend herself -- a psychical reparation.

JUST BUSINESS

Time and again patients seem unable to accept the conventional wisdom that the world of business is a cold and practical affair, wherein rudeness is not uncommon, the person gets lost in the shuffle, the art of empathy seems long forgotten, and the only bottom line is the mercenary one that calibrates profit and loss. To a surprising degree, they bring in to their sessions what to others might seem uneventful cut-and-dried instances of predictable impersonality: thus one man, in a fairly typical example, devoted much of his hour to an effort to understand why his simple request for follow-up information from a sales representative in a large urban department store was imperiously dispatched with -- "What! Get back to you? We're not a Ma and Pa family store, you know."

I would like to suggest that such instances of premeditated impersonality, if looked at from the standpoint of narcissistic giving, do not simply reflect the preoccupations of thin-skinned and troubled patients, but in fact point to a profound impairment in the ability to relate which evidences itself with particular clarity in the code of acceptable interpersonal transactions which has been generally adopted in the world of business.

Because such business behavior is part of the fabric of our daily lives, its deeper meaning is almost invariably overlooked: i.e., that under the guise of offering professionalism and the kind of objective attitude out of which supposedly useful information or relevant service might arise, a compelling rationalization is given for reacting in a manner so detached, informational, precise and functional that -- if it were to occur in any other conceivable social context -- it would sooner or later elicit the accusation or suspicion, "Why are you being so formal?" For this reason a concession is made to the American penchant for obligatory friendliness, and there is an attempt to relate in what might be called a personably impersonal way. Once again, the justification appears to be that in the business and professional world, where the purpose of the contact is presumably utilitarian and not social, the primary focus should be correspondingly on the practical aspects of the encounter (e.g., the purely private gratification one can derive from the transaction). In other words, the desires for intimacy which are always to some degree present, are to be jointly and tacitly relegated to the background and the relationship per se is to be manipulated for mutual self-interest.

Once again, what is ignored is that the basic existential need to have one's feelings affirmed, to have the other be, if not in attunement, at least aware of what one really wants, to continue to be validated as a unique person as opposed to an undistinguished unit of commerce -- even if momentarily subordinated to a functional purpose -- *never goes away*. And such needs are scarcely satisfied by the programmed friendliness and codified courtesies which pass for interacting in the business world. Not because they are put on the back burner, but because the vast majority of people do not know how to meet these needs for intimacy in the first place in the normal social context of ongoing interpersonal relations, and which, therefore, under the constrained conditions of professionalism and business etiquette, easily become neglected to a painful degree. (And in this sense, when people complain, as they frequently do, of consumer "rip-offs," they are, to a definite extent, finding a common scapegoat for a pervasive contemporary feeling that one is too often treated insensitively and indifferently by others in a variety of situations, both business and otherwise).

All of which is muddied by the fact that in the microcosm of business valid issues of relatedness are invariably intertwined with role requirements. This becomes especially clear if we take the basic psychoanalytic model of the mind -- id ,ego, superego -- and apply it to the function of role in a typical business transaction: in which case we would undoubtedly wind up assigning to it the psychical attributes of the ego (self-protective, reality-testing and adaptive) and the super-ego (conscience and ego ideal). What this means is that someone who wants to perform meritoriously as a legitimate businessman or businesswoman will aspire to be efficient, productive, reliable, and sufficiently ethical to engage the consumer's respect. Note however, that what has been left out of the catalogue of essential role requirements are any psychical characteristics pertaining to the id (e.g. spontaneous expression of real feelings and underlying attitude which the person performing the role has for the other). This creates an immediate problem because it is impossible to effectively eliminate the spontaneous, expressive, unconscious (id) part of the personality and the problem only becomes worse when there is an attempt, as there often is, to incorporate the id part into the role itself: i.e. to be obliged to playact that one likes and is really interested in every customer one encounters.

This is another way of saying that those interpersonal aspects of a business transaction and relationship, howsoever fleeting, that are real (non-role) cannot *therefore be pretended or role-played.* A role or technique cannot serve as a substitute because a role, even if primary, is always contained in the envelope of a real person who cannot avoid responding emotionally, unpredictably, and dynamically to whomever he engages, which cannot fail to evidence itself and to have at least some impact.

Now to return to our theme: the narcissistic-giving component in most business or professional transactions and relationships (including psychotherapy and psychoanalysis) is to believe that the necessity to be humanistically, existentially and empathically attuned to the other can somehow be either cancelled (as in business) or taken over by a technique or role (as in therapy). The narcissistic- giving component in a completely impersonal business relationship is to believe that by correctly relating in the prescribed politely attentive, friendly and efficient manner one has in effect discharged one's humanistic responsibility to be empathic and real and that there is no further need to relate to the person in any other way. What this often comes down to in business transactions, is the illusion that one can have no fundamental respect, interest, feeling, whatsoever, for the other, but as long as one covers it with courtesy and does not show it -- then one has *related* as well as need be. For this reason, people are not only quite sensitive to how they are treated in an everyday business transaction, but often use it as a hidden barometer of the degree to which they are respected by relative strangers. Their unconscious thinking perhaps being: if someone who doesn't have to think well of me (but needs only to pretend to), nevertheless, really does, then no doubt, he or she must be truly impressed; and, conversely -- since, in business, someone can get away with having no special regard for someone provided he or she is sufficiently polite and serviceable -- a person who truly does not think well of me is that much more likely to (covertly, beneath the politeness) show it. Which is why, as has been pointed out, consumer complaints are often protests about perceived blows to one's self-esteem disguising themselves as economic injustices one has allegedly suffered.

By contrast, being social, that is, playing a social role, is primarily about relating to and validating the self-esteem of the other and there is, supposedly, no functional purpose to the encounter as there is in business (unless, of course, one is trying to mix the two by networking). What is therefore called for here is not service or practical information, but a certain demonstrable enthusiasm for the person of the other. Such an enthusiastic display of interest in a comparative stranger or casual acquaintance is especially required at precisely those times when a person's self-esteem is most threatened: i.e., typically, upon greeting or saying good-bye to someone you have just met. Seen this way, being social means assuaging the natural anxiety upon encountering a stranger that you may either be hostilely rejected or, perceive, upon leaving, that the other is openly relieved to see you go. In large measure, being social therefore means acting as though one existentially welcomes the presence of the other (by carrying out a recognizable ceremony of reassurance that one is happy to make contact) and that one will miss the presence of the departing other (by performing a second ceremony which states that pleasure has been gained from the meeting). Being social means sharing an unspoken covenant with like-minded others who, as you, prefer not to have their feelings arbitrarily trampled on and therefore would rather create a safe environment wherein one can count on not being intentionally abused, shamed, rejected or painfully ignored. On an individual level, this may be the equivalent of the social contract between a people and their government which supposedly guarantees that one can walk the streets or go through daily life without unduly worrying that his or her constitutional liberties will be violated (that is, they will be protected if need be by either the police or the law).

Yet, if this is all that playing a social role psychologically means, if it is intended primarily to soothe our most primitive fears, if it is thereby directed to the most fragile part of our self-esteem and to nothing else, then being social -- like the government's being governmental -- by definition must be a superficial activity and a superficial way of relating. Or, to put it another way, from the standpoint of intimacy, nurturance and real relatedness, being social can at best be only a beginning: a safe ground is cleared for a potentially deeper relationship to develop, but whether or not two people will subsequently meaningfully connect, will have nothing to do with the preparatory social amenities. In part, this is because interactions which can be characterized as authentically intimate and nurturing, inasmuch as they must thereby contain a strong component of emotive spontaneity, *cannot be circumscribed in social conventions, roles, or techniques.*

And therefore the widespread belief that being social is being superficial and is no prognosticator of whether two individuals who have just met are going to become intimate, is well-founded. For this reason, people are justifiably uneasy once they have departed from the familiar harbor of playing a social role. After all, role-governed behavior, by its nature, is at least predictable; it has built-in constraints and it is shaped by abstract fantasies of how people generally wish to be treated and believe they are entitled to be treated. Role-governed behavior is not time-bound as is real, naturalistic or intimate behavior, which dynamically responds to the unpredictable moment (as well as to the personal, non role-bound unconscious of the other).

Social and business behavior are therefore alike in that both are role-governed, ahistorical and not real (in the sense of being interactively, intuitively plugged into the living moment) and to that extent are shallow. The narcissistic-giving element in both types of relating is the belief that somehow the performance of the role can be extrapolated so as to cover the most significant dimension of human transactions: i.e., to be in at least some kind of authentic attunement to the individual existential presence of the other. Which, by the way, has nothing to do with the desire or awareness of being interested in persuing a possible intimate bond with another. One can be intimate, although, of course, only briefly, even if one realizes that there is no intention to develop, or continue, the relationship with the person one has just encountered. Just as there is such a thing as a nurturing divorce or parting of the ways between a couple as opposed to a hostile separation (admittedly, the much more common scenario), there is a way to empathically resonate with the presence of a comparative or complete stranger that need not be dependent upon one's appraisal of the outcome of the interaction. Thus, even if one senses one would just as well not meet the person again, there is still time to intuit what the other is about, to affirm some aspect of his or her being, to keep an eye open for whatever personal meaning may be derived by either party and, by thereby being at least minimally attuned, to existentially validate the encounter in a manner that can never be encompassed in a technical or rote performance of the business, professional or social role.

To return now to my patient and his distress at being treated in a way that was not personal but, as the phrase goes, "just business." That phrase and what it connotes has been dramatically distorted in movies which romanticize the criminal lifestyle; wherein it has come to represent the ultimate in someone who is driven to psychopathically or psychotically carry out a professional code of conduct that can be so ruthlessly extreme it can confer the right to murder another person if that is what is necessary to implement one's more pressing ambitions. As uttered in the movies, at the appropriate dramatic moment, the phrase is meant to convey the most chillingly anti-human effect imaginable.

Yet, on a far more banal, legal, unnoticed and even socially sanctioned basis, the familiar process of completely turning away, tuning out, or refusing to be even minimally engaged with another person can be similarly covered up and rationalized under the banner of "just business." And in a sense, it can be more chilling, because real, to meet someone and to perceive, as is often the case, that outside of the personal advantage each aspires to gain from the other, there is no discernible trace of interest in any of the distinctive aspects of the self which to the person involved are most prized.

In that light, the narcissistic-giving component in such everyday business or professional transactions is the grandiose belief that efficient and productive impersonality can ever be a viable, let alone complete substitute for the fundamental need of the self to be confirmed in any interpersonal encounter, no matter how transient. Or to put it another way: to believe that by offering the benefits to be plausibly derived from an impersonal, professional or business relationship you have thereby delivered something of such value that the need to relate in a genuinely human way, can be justifiably suspended.

THE POLITICIZED PSYCHE

At almost the opposite end of the continuum from the patient who feels persecuted by the impersonality of "just business" relationships which seem to engulf him, is the person who insists on viewing nearly every detail of his or her daily existence as the offshoot of a complicated chain of political events. Because such people tend to see even their innermost psychical selves as politically shaped, I use the term *politicized psyche* to describe them. What follows is a common profile, drawn from a number of patients I have worked with. I offer it, in order to illuminate yet another dimension and instance of narcissistic giving. The most outstanding characteristic of the politicized psyche is its belief that everything that psychically occurs is somehow connected -- either as a by-product or direct target -- to a gigantic web of social interrelationships that is dynamically enveloping, infiltrating and transmuting society. Thus, no matter how hurt, trivialized or discounted one feels, there is the redeeming sense that one is, nevertheless, a part of a process, howsoever painful, that is meaningful. To a large intent, therefore, the politicized psyche replaces a self identity with a social identity (i.e., one whose main configurations have been internalized and particularized from external political events that have been deemed critically shaping for the social class or ethnic group with which the individual most powerfully identifies).

When the politicized psyche has a negative social identity (e.g., considers itself to be a member of an oppressed minority) which is often the case, then a solution is sought, not in changing the self, but in changing society. Since the assumption is that the root of the discontent is external, the normal superego self criticism and perceived failure to measure up to the ego ideal are more or less automatically projected onto the relevant social institutions which have been deemed culpable. Which places the politicized psyche in an immediate dilemma: on the one hand, relief is promised from the internal tension and wear and tear on the psyche engendered by a negative identity by deflecting anger and frustration away from the self and by mapping it onto society at large; but on the other hand, the realistic possibilities of converting such a negative social identity into a more positive one through the strategy of seeking to actively implement, or merely to just wait for, the required social upheavals -- are almost nil. On some level, the politicized psyche not only knows this but even manages to score points with itself by using the long odds against rehabilitating a corrupt social order as proof that one has earned at least a kind of honorary psychical red badge of courage. Thus, the politicized psyche derives much of its self-esteem -- not through individual, concrete accomplishments (after all, no one person can be expected to, or be blamed for failing to right society's wrongs) -- but from this admirable adoption of a David-versus-Goliath identity.

It follows from this that the politicized psyche can act out with impunity because it sees itself as a splendid lone wolf protestor against an unjust society;

44

and in such a context of oppressive social crisis acting out becomes, not unrestrained self-indulgence, but the responsible enactment of a troubled social conscience. With much the same rationalization, feelings of rage and contempt can be freely ventilated and retrospectively justified by pointing to the magnitude of the social crimes against which they are purportedly targeted. And similarly, overreacting, bursts of excessive emotionality, fits of hysteria can be explained away as the by-products and understandable fallout of a state of abnormal psychical strain produced by a pathologically depriving and unconscionably indifferent society.

In addition, the politicized psyche substitutes for the regular interpersonal dyad, the romantic situation of the individual pitted against a repressive political regime. When this is the case, it is easy to see that interpersonal relationships on the whole are forced to become more abstract, impersonal and rigidly defined (because politically restricted). Moreover, the person tends to be emotively reactive: i.e., if how you feel depends, not on your frame of mind when you start out the day, but on what the newspapers or media tell you about that part of current affairs you are especially interested in -- then you can not help but feel passive. And when things go wrong -- since, being viewed globally, they can assume the proportions of large scale disasters -- it is natural to feel persecuted; and, again, since it is not one person, but massive social collectives, who are persecuting you it is not farfetched to believe you are being conspired against.

The politicized psyche is thus vulnerable to paranoia, but it is difficult to recognize and deal with such paranoia, because if the designated enemy is an inhumane social institution or an oppressive governmental body (e.g., the police force) then, by virtue of the laws of probability pertaining to large numbers, there are bound to be numerous confirming instances of whatever persecutory trauma one is on the lookout for. From a psychological standpoint, therefore, the politicized psyche will typically lack the structure of a cohesive ego, if only because it tends to base its reality testing on the slippery foundation of the ebb and flow of large scale political events. By contrast, the reality testing of the ordinary non-politicized psyche -- although also resting on the unpredictable changes of everyday life -- will be considerably more reliable inasmuch as it will basically restrict itself to those contingencies upon which the individual ego has the best chance of impacting, and, therefore, of partially controlling. Thus, comparatively speaking, the reality-testing of the politicized psyche (often to a pathological degree) will be less structured and more provisional.

For all of these reasons, when it comes to personal relating, partners will be looked upon as potential personifications of principles and political viewpoints, rather than as constellations of unique psychical forces, and compatibility of ideas or politics will be preferred over compatibility of personalities. How one votes or how one thinks, therefore, often becomes far more important than how one relates, which does not mean, however, that politicized-psyche relationships are essentially cerebral, ideological partnerships: in point of fact they can be intensely, volatively emotional, but the emotions will seem to pivot on momentous politicized ideas that are thought to hold the key to the future of mankind (they themselves being but the actors in an historical drama which transcends the significance of the individual players). When this is carried to the extreme case, when two like-minded politicized psyches join in a relationship, they may actually experience themselves, not as lovers, but as underground cell members or diehard comrades in a great and glorious cause.

Finally, it should be clear by now, that the narcissistic-giving component in such cases is to believe that by politicizing the psyche one is somehow offering another person something far greater, more meaningful, committed and richer than a simple, one-on-one human relationship that is based on a reciprocal and profound intimacy.

THEY HAVE THE POWER

Anyone who has worked intensively with struggling young artists, as I have, quickly comes to realize, if he doesn't already know it, what it means to perceive oneself as powerless. Only perhaps an artist who happens to be an actor can work for months or years developing a monologue or preparing for a role and then suffer the humiliation of having it appraised and summarily dismissed, typically within just minutes, by either an agent or casting director. Only a performing artist, let us say a cabaret singer, can devote a solid year towards perfecting her act and then discover sometimes in the course of a single evening, that, so far as the audience is concerned, "It does not work." And only an aspiring concert pianist, someone who may have arduously studied ten years in order to reach a certain virtuoso level, can enter a prestigious international competition, and be told at the conclusion of an audition that may last less than an hour, that one simply does not possess the requisite tools or talent to make it.

The common denominator in all such cases of unequivocal, painful and swift dashing of one's hopes (certainly highlighted, but by no means restricted to aspiring artists) is the sense of psychic impotence often expressed in the contemporary lament, "The have the power." What this refers to is the situation wherein two people are supposedly engaged in arriving at an important decision, which, however, primarily affects one person, but where the person who *should* have the power, has almost none. Thus, to take an extreme example, a composer can submit a life's work to an established critic, who, if he or she chooses, can demolish it in less than a hundred words. When this occurs, there is, of course, not only no dialogue but a vast and unbearable inequity of investment: on the one hand, there is the person who has committed perhaps thousands of days to a cherished project, who therefore should have the deciding vote, but doesn't; and, on the other hand, there is the authority with designated power, who can decimate with impunity whatever crosses its path (via rejection) almost instantaneously.

Having no power is therefore equivalent to experiencing one's psychical autonomy or executive ego function in an area of choice that is crucial to one's self-esteem as being cruelly externalized and unfairly appropriated by an alien ego: not out of ill will or hostility (although it can often be experienced that way if the narcissistic injury becomes palpable enough to trigger a paranoid sense of being persecuted) but, typically, because someone simply has the power to do it. That there are certain characteristic, socially sanctioned situations and roles which reinforce this impression -- e.g. a doctor examining an x-ray or laboratory blood test report who in seconds can prognosticate on the probable longevity of an individual's life; a jury deciding whether a defendant should be set free or imprisoned; a judge deliberating on what sentence shall be passed -- is terrifying. The fact that there are clear-cut social symbols, pertaining to daily transactions, wherein people often experience themselves as vitally involved yet personally powerless and must defer to the external authority of an individual, a convention or an organization, creates endless resentment: to take just one example think of someone who considers a particular food item to be outrageously overpriced and would love to refuse to pay for it, but feels he or she cannot afford for reasons of health not to buy the product.

Now, since many political, economic or legal requirements are made for the benefit of a specific group, large or small, *but never for the needs of the individual*, there will be therefore countless times when people -- who are forced to submit to interpersonal transactions that were obviously not created for their benefit -- will experience narcissistic injury as a result of the customs, conventions and rules of society. The narcissistic giving component lies in society's justification that somehow, by serving the collective, they are also serving the individual; and, while it is highly debatable whether that were ever the case, what does seem clear is that the application of social power (whether by judge, businessman, editor, or doctor) is essentially employed for the advantage of the user and not the recipient. (The sociologist, Erving Goffman, has brilliantly explored the multifarious ways in which people attempt to manipulate a variety of social roles, for the sole purpose of obtaining power over others.)

Living socially, therefore, to a great extent can be characterized as living for the statistical benefit of others, and this is immediately brought home whenever there is a clash between what one feels one is socially or legally obliged to do and what one really wants to do. Even customs, rules or laws that are supposedly designed to protect or enhance the inalienable human or civil rights of the private person are of necessity so conceived with the generalized, statistical or abstract individual in mind and this once again becomes painfully apparent in the universal everyday experience of it being rare whenever the specific social, economic, or legal requirement seems to comfortably (let alone exactly) fit the unique needs of the individual.

Thus, one almost always feels that something is occurring too soon, too late, too much, with one or another quality invariably askew so as to persistently reinforce the deflating feeling that it is the *needs of the collective social individual and never you that are being catered to.*

So far, we have been considering the numerous occasions wherein there is a glaring inequity of power, when it seems that the one who should have the power, does not, but that "they have the power." Yet, there is a different and perhaps even more common scenario: the situation in which two people feel sufficiently well-matched to engage in a "power struggle." Generally, before this can erupt, certain preconditions will have been fulfilled: a state of mutual mistrust, or even paranoia, will have been reached wherein each party will have no hope of receiving even minimal nurturance from the other, but will feel that whatever one gets, one will have to fight for. Moreover, each will feel that the other is not only non-giving, but is greedy in an intrusive way, wanting to appropriate something that does not properly belong to the other. A power struggle comes to be, therefore, when a relationship has been reduced to only a matter of psychic force, strategy and coercion. Traditionally, it is fought out in the open, each side trotting out its psychological arsenal as a show of strength and as a warning. By contrast, the power struggle of the person who is termed clinically paranoid will be characteristically covert, the experience being much closer to that of a spy or secret agent.

What the person interlocked in a power struggle seems to be striving for (in the name of self-preservation) is a defense of psychical home turf as one views it, which typically takes the form of a vigorous and angry definition of one's boundaries. One wants, in this case, respect and not love. Or, to put it more accurately, one becomes convinced that there cannot be love without first respect and that perhaps -- since anyone who experiences himself or herself as entangled in a power struggle with someone else clearly does not feel loved -- what is therefore missing is the ingredient of necessary respect, which, if earned, may then be followed by love. Yet, since the respect one gains from winning a power struggle is invariably tainted with the fear and humiliation of the recently vanquished, it is unconsciously equated with the kind of respect regularly paid to the successful bully: it is the homage that is elicited not by nurturance (which is always freely given) but is coerced by instilling a dread of the consequences which would come from *not* respecting the person (further bullying which may escalate, should the bully become narcissistically enraged, to outright terrorizing tactics).

By contrast with the respect which is freely given in response to an experience of being nurtured, someone who attempts to gain deference through intimidation, at best gets a pretense: one acts *as if* one respects in order to avoid punitive consequences. And since two people locked in a power struggle have, by definition, surrendered any realistic hope of being validated in a nurturing way, force will seem to be the strategy of choice. Which is why such individuals often perceive themselves as, and in fact most resemble, psychic policemen and policewomen: each has the duty to protect one's rightful personal boundaries, with force if necessary, since it is obvious they are not likely to be respected in any other way.

Finally, the narcissistic-giving component is to delude oneself that the respect purchased through triumphant power brokering is in any measure genuine; that the resultant relationship, no matter how close, can ever contain intimacy; and that somehow, by proving your superior strength, you are thereby giving the other something of value.

CHARACTERISTICS OF NARCISSISTIC GIVING

Perhaps the most salient characteristic to emerge from a study of examples of narcissistic giving, is the rapid, almost impulsive nature of the transaction. Typically, a narcissistic-giving response is delivered (and finished with) in a flash. Thus, a woman, who has been out of work for three months and who has not heard for over a week from the counselor at the employment agency with which she has registered, anxiously telephones for possible news and is instantly told, "Someone will get back to you." Or, as was the case with my patient, a very intelligent, ambitious young social worker who had submitted to his boss a multifaceted, intricately worked out proposal to enhance the efficiency of the agency they both worked for and who -- after receiving not a single word of feedback in over six months -- finally inquired if it had ever been read at all and was immediately told: "It's right here on my desk." Such speed of reply, of course, cannot be coincidental and what it points to (via omission and reversal) is the simple but profound fact that real giving is a process which takes some time, while narcissistic giving, by contrast, is a non-process impulsive defense meant to shore up a shaky self-esteem that is notably fragile when it comes to the issue of nurturing another person. Narcissistic-giving responses, as is true of narcissistic responses in general, are characteristically brief in part because they are tailored for the needs of just one person, and are, therefore, inherently less complicated than a genuinely interpersonal interaction which has to take two people into account. And this is even more true of narcissistic giving which is usually precipitated by a kind of panic that one is on the brink of being exposed for being incapacitated when it comes to empathically addressing the needs of the other -- a panic which has the effect of hastening the reply in an attempt to nip the anxiety in the bud by imposing a premature closure on a situation that is anything but resolved.

Not surprisingly, the receiver of such a narcissistic-giving response is often left with the unpleasant feeling that, somehow, the rug has been deftly pulled out from under him or her. While simultaneously, from the perspective of the narcissistic giver, there is the expectation, and the message is imparted, that the transaction is all over with and it is time to move on. There is a sense, therefore, in which responses such as, "Someone will get back to you," and, "It's right here on my desk," are designed to deliver the latent threat, "Are you satisfied?"; and this becomes painfully clear should the auditor resist the patently false closure that has been offered and persist in repeating the original request (which then, typically, gets greeted with an impatient burst of indignation, experienced by the narcissistic giver as narcissistic injury).

Since narcissistic giving is denoted by an underlying, fragile impatience it naturally strives for expeditious resolution which it tries to achieve through the strategy of oversimplification and concretization. For this reason, narcissistic givers are inordinately fond of reducing complicated emotional requests which often hinge on multi-determined dynamic and often unconscious forces to the status of pedestrian one-dimensional questions, as though a complex, conflictual human need could ever be satisfied with the dispensing of prosaic information (e.g., regarding time or logistics).

Other important characteristics in addition to impulsive speed of reply, are:

1.   Sleight of hand. Since narcissistic givers cannot and do not intend to meet the legitimate needs of the other, they use the concrete, in the manner of a magician, as a sleight-of-hand distraction. And to that degree, they are not merely indirect, they are willfully diversionary.

2.   Subversive. They seek to defuse whatever urgency there may be to the supplicant's situation, by devaluing the nature of the demand. Thus, there is often a palpable note of mockery in their responses, and a kind of derisive, "So, what's all the fuss about?"

3.   Bullying. They are not above exploiting the vulnerability and neediness of the other, whom they typically attempt to coerce into accepting a grossly sub-par gratification.

4.   Pseudo-logical. Since they tend to shun insight and introspection, at least in the sensitive area pertaining to their narcissistic giving, they endeavor to reduce complex interpersonal transactions to matters of syllogistic logic: thereby denying unconscious motivation and aiming to boil down thorny relational issues to cut-and-dried questions of conscious problem solving. The assumption, therefore, is that the matter at hand is one of alternative choices to a simple dilemma, and the latent intimidation is that if one does not readily acquiesce to the narcissistic-giving solution

which has been superficially presented, then one is either (a) ungrateful or (b) incompetent.

5.   False Self. Since narcissistic giving invariably denies unconscious conflict or vulnerability of any kind and, in effect, relies upon a hastily contrived defensive facade, it may be characterized as a quintessential false self (as has been delineated by the great psychoanalyst, D.W. Winnicott). And this is another way of saying that a narcissistic-giving response is one that is bent upon revealing as little as possible, or, more precisely, the exact opposite of the true self.

WHEN SHAME GOES PUBLIC

Most of the examples so far presented have been drawn from the lower, everyday end of the continuum of narcissistic giving. At the extreme upper end are what might be called public confessions of hitherto-suppressed shameful traumas that are clearly offered as corrective emotional experiences. This is not, of course, to devalue the importance of peer group support, therapeutic confession, looking squarely in the eye a past victimhood, and so on. It is to say, that from the standpoint of narcissistic giving, it is quite easy, and therefore tempting, to appear to be giving oneself fully to others by courageously revealing a previously, carefully-hidden shame. Someone, for example, who actually goes on national television, whether as a celebrity daring to be shockingly vulnerable or as an everyman who has decided to come forth, can thereby seem: to be much more honest than the average person who, as we all know, typically calls upon a host of face-saving maneuvers just to get through the day's routines; to be much more principled, inasmuch as one is willing to stake a reputation that may have taken a lifetime to build up on a single, seemingly profound existential decision that it is necessary to expose a personal shame in the hope of alerting an apathetic public to an overlooked but widespread civic threat; and, finally, because of this, to be much deeper and more authentic than the ordinary person who will hardly risk anything personally valuable to further a political cause or help out a needy stranger (Kitty Genovese syndrome) and will characteristically pursue self-interest, even in an event as historic as the recent presidential election (i.e., by "voting their pocketbook").

For all of these reasons, someone who voluntarily accepts the dangers to one's self-esteem that can follow upon airing out the greatest of all family skeletons (e.g. incest) before the broadest of all possible audiences (e.g. a nationally syndicated TV talk show) cannot help but take on the aura of a larger-than-life character, a person heroically public-spirited and astonishingly unafraid to imperil basic narcissistic self-interests. And, indeed, this does seem to be the role to which most public confessors aspire.

When I say that it is easy to appear to be giving oneself fully by courageously revealing a shameful trauma from the past, I do not mean to thereby underestimate the difficulty required in actually following this through: on the contrary, it takes definite fortitude, that -- depending on the magnitude of the confession -- can verge on a bravado that few of us could muster, even if we wanted to. But what I do wish to point out is that real giving, what could be called in this circumstance intimate disclosure, involves much more than the revelation of a deep dark secret (especially a deep dark secret that has a certain trendy, built-in approval rating). Intimate disclosure, by contrast, is a fundamental component of ongoing intimacy -- the foundation, to take just one example, of the indispensable capacity to reveal oneself within the professional frame of psychotherapy -- but it far transcends the simple, howsoever dramatic telling of painful, horrible secrets.

In fact, as I believe most psychotherapists would agree, what carries greater significance, and is therefore more revealing, is not *what* the secret is, but *why* and *how* the secret was kept. As compared with narcissistic-giving disclosure, intimate disclosure is a *process* rather than a one-time, cathartic experience and from this perspective, telling a secret is only the *beginning*. This is because intimate disclosure involves, among other things, assuming responsibility for the so-called secret one has just told and, accordingly, does not stop with the telling, but usually goes on to reflect on why the secret was kept, its meaning and the consequences that ensued from its suppression. Because of this, someone who intimately discloses, is often as interested in the ramifications upon the feelings of her auditor for the sake of the auditor's own feelings, as opposed to the typical public confessor's insatiable curiosity as to how her secret has gone over with her chosen audience.

What this means, is that someone who intimately discloses does so in the hope of drawing closer to another person. This is very different from the narcissistic-giving disclosure which characteristically first searches for the proper audience with which to achieve the desired exhibitionistic release. For this reason, a narcissistic-giving confession tends to be structured along the lines of a theatrical performance and the dynamics of the relationship it pursues are more likely to be what one might expect from a performing artist and an audience rather than from a reciprocally intimate transaction between two people who are capable of nurturing and of being nurtured. This is particularly clear in the case of individuals who choose to publicize their traumatic childhood secrets -- they are the children of alcoholics, children of abusive and molesting parents, children of narcissists -- where, by definition of the interpersonal situation they are setting up, there is virtually no chance for the listener to in any way meaningfully respond, let alone interact. Because once the great secret is told in the manner deemed best suited to mobilize the most sympathetic and public-spirited reaction, the relationship as such is over -- not to be resumed until someone new is found to whom to tell the great secret. And in that respect, they could be called *confessional Don Juans.*

In the course of conducting over one thousand diagnostic intake interviews over a seven year span, in addition to being in private practice as a psychotherapist for nearly fifteen years, I have had the opportunity to observe a number of survivors of childhood abuse of one form or another, who had reached the point of finally having come to terms with both the fact of their shame-inducing abuse and their concomitant need to confront someone (usually the parent or sibling who either perpetrated the abuse, or -- often equally or even more complicitous in the mind of victim -- who colluded by failing to *protect* the helpless child). Nevertheless, as I have stressed, such intimate disclosure and subsequent responsible confrontation with the (typically) hotly-denying abuser -- necessary as they are to eventual mental health recovery -- are but a first step. Much more decisive is whether this first step leads to the beginning of an arduous journey of committed self-discovery which will, among other things, take personal responsibility -- not so much for being a victim, but for being shaped by its aftermath.

A trauma, no matter how dissociated, repressed or split-off in the ego, is always, to some degree, gradually integrated with the remainder of the non-traumatized psyche and how this is done is always specific and therefore reveals a great deal about the choices of the individual. Yet, it is often this crucial part -- how the rest of the personality reacted to the trauma -- that is left conspicuously uninvestigated by certain gung ho trauma hunters of the recovery movement that is currently in vogue. And frequently the centerpiece of their treatment will hinge on the ventilation and psychic expulsion of the designated repressed childhood trauma. Which is especially evident in the otherwise moving writings of Alice Miller, where one gets the impression that once the childhood pain of being abused by one's parents is somehow fully acknowledged, felt and abreacted, therapy comes to a close. In my view, as I've made clear, that is where it begins.

As the psychoanalyst, David Shapiro, has shown, regardless of how devastating a childhood trauma may have been, no one person is composed of just a traumatic nuclear conflict and a system of defense against it. People and their psyches are more complicated than that which is why I believe it does little good to confer upon a plainly suffering individual a "victim" identity (e.g. children of alcoholic, narcissistic, abusive parents) if only because it opens up broad avenues for narcissistic giving expression and satisfying, but shallow gratification.

THE MAGIC OF SOAPS

Unless one has fallen under the spell of televised daytime soap operas or has listened to patients (as I have) who are so enamored, it is difficult to comprehend let alone not outright laugh at their supposed influence. Yet, after taking quite seriously and exploring a sufficient number of my patients' fantasies revolving around the vicissitudes of their respective soap heroes and heroines, I do not doubt the veracity of the incident I recently heard reported on talk radio: a group of late-night party-goers had been accosted in Central Park by a mugger with a gun who then proceeded to systematically rob each person. Upon coming up to an elderly, distinguished-looking man (whom he apparently recognized as a protagonist in a leading daytime soap) the mugger stopped short, patted him on the shoulder, said, "Not you. You're my story (i.e. he faithfully watches him) and then went on to rob the person who was next in line.

I suggest this is a curious phenomenon worthy of an explanation. Putting aside the intricate web of expectations, fantasies and identifications people regularly project onto their favorite soap "stories," one way to understand their incredible contemporary appeal is to view them as holding the mirror up to nature in terms of just what it is that we find appealing and entertaining in the compass of our daily lives (a subject I deal with more fully in Chapter Three). And in such an interpersonal context, soaps show, as perhaps no other media does, the degree to which what is accepted as gratification in real life relationships, can be directly explained as instances of narcissistic giving.

If this is so, then what are the narcissistic-giving features of relationships which are portrayed in serialized soap operas? Here are some of the more important ones:

1. Their central issues are invariably melodramatically larger than life: i.e. typically, betrayal, seduction, abandonment, manipulation, ruthless competition, murderous rage, rape, terminal illness, etc. The implication is that the conflicts being presented are significantly more interesting than those of everyday life; or, to put it another way, that the naturally slower rhythms of a genuinely intimate relationship are somehow less meaningful and dramatically engaging than the emotional fireworks regularly dished out to loyal fans.

2. By their studied omission of anything realistically complicated, subdued or thoughtfully mature, soaps further imply that what people will respond to most as spectator audience are only those aspects of their personal lives that are capable of being sensationalized. What this means on another level is that people are considered as being unable to sustain interest in authentic relating and require, instead, a greatly speeded-up version of what might be called relational highlights. And since people are believed to be so impatient to be gratified that they are willing to bypass entirely the organic flow of a relationship in order to hurry on to the conclusion or payoff, the lives of soap characters are presented essentially as a series of titillating outcomes. In turn, what is considered titillating are prototypical, fantastically stressful situations that have seemingly worn down the inner controls of protagonists, as a result of which pathological acting out, either subtly or grossly, has began to unfold.

Therefore, while soaps traditionally abound, even revel in conflicts, these are not the conflicts of intimacy, which generally hinge on the capacity, on the one hand, for reciprocal nurturing and, on the other, on the attendant anxieties concerning incorporation, transgression or dissolution of one's boundaries, and the paranoid fear of the dangers ensuing from too much closeness. By contrast, soap conflicts are those of the desperado (i.e. sooner or later they reach crisis proportions): e.g., do I reveal my despicable betrayal and thereby lose my fortune, or do I stay involved with someone whom I can't stand? They are conflicts that are founded on the clash between inordinate, often sociopathic self-interest and the forces in the immediate environment which sooner or later are raised in opposition. Seen this way, what gets dramatized in soaps, is the sometimes spectacular excitement that can be stirred up by the depiction of *non-intimate* relationships that are enacted as boldly, forcefully, and pathologically as possible.

3.   The episodic, theatrical excitement of the roller-coaster lifestyles of soap characters can serve as a manic defense (in the sense of D.W. Winnicott) to cover up the absence of aliveness and boredom that are the concomitants of the intimacy void that is prevalent in today's world.

For all of these reasons, soaps provide an excellent opportunity to study contemporary relationships from the standpoint of what it is that specifically constitutes non-intimacy.

Some of the most significant non-intimate components include:

1.   The overvaluing and pursuit of sensation in relationships which are primarily viewed as means for the achievements of exciting experiences.

2.   Conflicts and issues almost invariably being acted out. There does not seem to be such a thing as a concept of delay of gratification.

3.   Characters, as soon as they are in touch with a conflict, becoming gripped by the urgency of their needs. A corrective sense of interpersonal mutuality is notably missing.

4.   Characters showing scant self-awareness or insight into the motives of the other, but expending most of their energy on finding expedient ways to gratify their usually pressing desires.

5.   The philosophy of Machiavellianism being substituted for the practice of honestly negotiating and endeavoring to work through substantive relational differences.

6.   Relationships, accordingly, being appraised -- not for their power to nurture -- but, objectively, from the standpoint of projected results. Did one or can one get what one wanted, or still wants? In such a view, human partnerships are seen as psychological lotteries, wherein players scheme to invest as little as possible, while hoping to make a personal killing in terms of what they get back.

7.   The excitement therefore offered in soaps being that of the hunt. The prospect of intriguing characters on the brink of gratifying themselves beyond their most thrilling dreams, is constantly dangled.

8.   Finally, the fact that absent in all this, is what Bion referred to as the capacity to tolerate frustration, depression and the pain intrinsic to emotional development.

Since the characters in soaps, as relational beings, are profoundly non-intimate it is not surprising that typically the event and situation seem more important than the people. The protagonists, while meant to be dramatically interesting, are only so because their desperate attempts to extricate themselves from assorted crises are voyeuristically compelling; but not because their internal conflicts are in any real sense powerfully in-depth or dynamically engaging. For this reason, characters in soaps, to some extent like characters in action movies, are conceived as containers in which prototypcially dramatic scenarios (e.g. betrayal, seduction, rape, murder, car crashes, etc.) are enacted. Without such enlivening scenarios, they are quite uninteresting.

What soaps do, then, is to transform the action of action films into the relational realm of supposedly everyday people. The result is a new experiential genre -- what might be called *action relationships*. This is why stories move so fast in soaps and it is one of the ways attention is deflected away from how uninteresting and emotionally impoverished, as people, the lead characters are. Accordingly, relationships are literally always *moving*.

This, of course, is in marked contrast to intimate relationships where there is, of necessity, numerous occasions for rest and down time (if only to process the complex thoughts and feelings that invariably arise). The basic technique by which soaps achieve their accelerated pace -- a fictional manic defense against the underlying deadness and absence of intimacy -- is probably suspense: i.e., when someone is locked into paying unremitting attention to a well-chosen dramatic scenario that has been designed to stir up so much anxiety over the outcome that the enmeshed spectator feels compelled to wait it out. Suspense is therefore a state in which every moment will seem anything but boring, and thereby significant, inasmuch as it produces fingernail-biting tension which begs to be relieved. Because of this, suspense has the function of switching off the critical observing ego (the part of the psyche, for example, that might notice and be distressed by the fact that the protagonist of the suspense-inducing drama is actually someone who, if his or her back were not perpetually up against the wall, would hardly enlist our interest or respect); and is therefore an indispensable strategic ploy of directors of action movies or producers of daytime TV soap operas who, by the nature of the medium they are working in, are routinely confronted with the task of inducing audiences to become involved with essentially uninteresting people -- or rather people who are only interesting to the extent that they enact their life scripts considerably more sociopathically, narcissistically and pathologically than the average person. Suspense is therefore in contrast to intimacy where -- while there may be surprise -- there is typically meaningful discovery, developmental unfolding and a cohesive sense of process.

I suggest this is important because it indicates that what people find entertaining and exciting in their daily lives -- that is, immediate gratification, overstimulation and sensationalism -- are unquestionably elements of narcissistic giving. In terms of soap operas, the critical narcissistic-giving component is overstimulation: i.e., by stimulating someone to a degree beyond the normal capacity to meaningfully respond, it creates the illusion on the one hand that the person is receiving far more than he or she could possibly expect; while simultaneously diverting attention, on the other hand -- through the crude but effective maneuver of preoccupying the spectator with an overload of excitation -- away from the underlying poverty of nurturance and absence of relational substance. And in the world of daytime TV soaps, the classic overstimulation is suspense.

By contrast, there is a kind of entertainment or deep gratification and satisfaction to be derived from an intimate relationship and from its dramatic counterpart -- a work of art. As does an intimate relationship, a work of art satisfies, gratifies and entertains, but such pleasures are more likely to be the aftermath rather than the goal. Unlike the soap, an authentic work of art aims to induct its audience into an aesthetically intimate relationship with its protagonist and this is so even if the fictional hero or heroine is someone who plainly cannot relate: i.e., someone who may be sociopathic, narcissistic or schizoid. It is accomplished by the fact that, in the case of the true work of art, the audience senses that the author always maintains an intimate and profound connection to his protagonist, even if his protagonist is incapable of intimacy: in other words, the authorial aesthetic perspective is always one of intimacy and depth, so that if the central character, for example, is pathologically incapable of maintaining a meaningful connection with another human being (as, of course, is true of many contemporary anti-heroes) then all the poignancy and pathos of such an emotional handicap will be especially and vividly portrayed. Needless to say, this is the opposite attitude of the soaps where the psychopathy and narcissism of its players are invariably milked for its sensationalism.

Yet, if this is so, if it is the intimacy in a real life relationship and its aesthetic dramatic equivalent in a work of art that most deeply satisfies and that ultimately entertains (in the sense of providing meaningful, non-ephemeral pleasure) -- then why is it, as I have tried to show, that so much narcissistic giving abounds? Which is like asking why is it that so many more people watch daytime TV soaps rather than seek out great films or read great novels and why is it that so many more people pursue relationships that are based on narcissistic giving rather than on reciprocal, empathic nurturance? This is a vast question, to which much of the rest of the book may be seen to address itself, but for a start, let me point to something so obvious that it is often overlooked: it is much easier to allow oneself to be caught up in the almost instant gratifications, the never-ending titillations and the sensationalistic payoffs of soaps than to immerse oneself in even a portion of the gruelling mental and emotional spade work that nearly every deep work of art eventually demands of its audience, in order to be truly known. (In this respect, it can be said that the relationship of a genuine work of art to its audience, as is the case in an authentic human partnership, is reciprocal: i.e., the work of art not only symbolically gives, but it requires a psychical investment on the part of the audience. We, therefore, immediately see, as one salient characteristic of superficial, narcissistic-giving art -- that it fosters a non-reciprocal, asymmetrical relationship in which the audience (e.g. TV soap opera fan) is encouraged, through seductive promises of surefire gratification to be completely and safely passive).

And, finally, it is easier to become involved in a relationship that similarly promises short-term gratifications and predictable, swiftly attainable pleasures than to try to cope with and to pursue the elusive, generally delayed, far more risky -- but for that reason incomparably more profound, satisfying and even entertaining -- rewards intrinsic to the type of human bonding characterized by intimacy.

CHAPTER TWO

Strategies of Narcissistic Giving

AN INTERPERSONAL DEFENSE

In order to show how prevalent narcissistic giving is, I began the first chapter with an explanation of why it is such a universal defense. In this chapter, in order to show how frequently narcissistic giving becomes the basis for various strategies of relating, I would like to begin with a discussion of why it is an interpersonal defense.

To do that, it may be helpful to remember what it is that the defense of narcissistic giving is defending against. There is this basic scenario: someone who generally has come to feel notably deficient when faced with the fact of nurturing, empathizing with or relating to a specified need perceived as outside the sphere of familiar self-interests; who is confronted with an unexpected or unwanted request for assistance that is typically rationally presented and thereby difficult to deny without exposing the underlying fragility of the capacity to give; and who responds with a kind of stopgap grandiose bluff which (for a variety of reasons which have been duly noted) works amazingly well. There are in this basic scenario at least three important elements, each of which is capable of drastically lowering self-esteem: one, the activation of the hidden "basic fault" in the area of nurturing another person; two, the potentially shame-inducing but unavoidable interpersonal situation calling for at least a minimal ability to relate (and thereby threatening to expose its absence); and three, the resultant defense which is little more than a makeshift display of pretentious acting out.

It is because narcissistic giving is a transaction which always involves at least one other person that I call it an interpersonal defense. There are significant differences between an interpersonal defense and an intrapsychic one. Perhaps most fundamental, is that in a classical intrapsychic defense such as repression, denial, rationalization or obsessional rumination, the threat (ultimately) comes essentially from within the self, as opposed to a defense such as narcissistic giving where there is the added component of having to deal with someone else. So, for example, if a disturbing thought or feeling is in danger of breaking through the protective barrier of ordinary repression, there is basically only the person's own psyche to combat it; whereas in an interpersonal defense there is also an other who may not only be closely watching the person's reactions but who often may have partially instigated it, thereby having a direct stake in the outcome. In this sense an interpersonal defense is doubly reinforced (two superegos watching) and, as a result, has some distinctive characteristics: it is more provisional, pragmatic, hasty and sometimes even chaotic due to the fact--since there is so much less time in which to process what is happening--it has to evolve in the crucible of a here and now interaction, and this is true even if the essential pattern is repeated thousands of times in the course of a lifetime. An interpersonal defense is therefore open-ended because it must leave room for possible responses of the other. (In biological language, an intrapsychic defense can be thought of as more of a closed program and an interpersonal defense as more of an *open* program, inasmuch as greater learning is involved.)

By comparison, a traditional intrapsychic defense such as repression (which may, of course, be repeatedly strengthened by the interactive influence of interpersonal education) will still have considerably more time in which to evolve in relative isolation and will accordingly operate at quite a different pace. Now, while there is no such thing as an intrapsychic or interpersonal defense in pure isolation (both being variously and continuously intermixed) the definition of an interpersonal defense will pertain to cases in which the defensive function is activated in a dyadic situation as opposed to an intrapsychic defense which will be utilized primarily for the self's relations with the self, most of which will occur privately. If this is so, an interpersonal defense such as narcissistic giving will almost naturally tend towards acting out, be less stable, less structured, less under the control of the solitary ego and more subject to direct social pressures, role performance anxiety and social reality-testing as opposed to an intrapsychic defense such as repression which will be governed more silently and internally by the superego (especially the ego ideal).

Perhaps one brief example can illustrate and bring to life the crucial difference between an intrapsychic and an interpersonal defense. Imagine someone with a certain obsessional train of thought (e.g., fantasying about turning the tables on one's enemies) which, whenever anxious, can be safely played back to oneself as a means of substitutive self-assuagement. Now imagine that, unexpectedly--while engaged in this ritualistic fantasy of secretly vindicating oneself--another person appears. It immediately becomes apparent that the private but ongoing obsessional train of thought (even if it happened to include an internalized dialogue of sorts with a second party) must at once give way to the contingent stimuli of a separate person's thoughts and feelings which, by the nature of their separation, are subject to never-ending uncertainty. What this means is that if one now wishes to continue--in the presence of this other--to exercise a comparable defensive control and ritualistic assuagement of one's anxiety by engaging in private obsessional thinking (e.g., savoring the details of an imaginary revenge) then, to a minimal extent, a whole range of complicated and unknown thoughts and feelings of the other must be factored in (in order to at least keep up the facade of normally relating). It follows that whatever prior defensive tasks had been posed to the solitary self have been vastly compounded by the addition of just one more person (and this is true even if the interrupted self resorts to the radical escape mechanism of schizoid withdrawal). From this point of view, the difference between an intrapsychic and an interpersonal defense is similar to the difference between a rehearsal and an improvisation, between a taped performance and a live one: an intrapsychic defense being more like a private inner self that one can tinker with and try to perfect in solitude while an interpersonal defense will call for a public response of one kind or another.

Because it is necessarily sensitive to the vicissitudes of group dynamics, it is a salient characteristic of an interpersonal defense that it will, over time, evolve into a strategy: that is, something which endeavors (like a psychical military battle plan) to allow for the contingencies of an unspecified number of imaginary adversaries. A strategic interpersonal defense such as narcissistic giving will therefore be forced to calculate crude statistical averages or probabilities of behavioral reactions in others as opposed to the more monolithic, reflex-like action of a primary intrapsychic defense such as repression. This type of strategy will tend to be goal-oriented, being constrained to cope with a material threat in the shape of an imminent other. It will be more behavioral, being obviously unable to settle its conflicts or achieve its aims on a strictly internal basis. (This behavioral component is perhaps the clearest difference between an intrapsychic and interpersonal defense.) And, by the nature of the live opposition it faces, it will be more game-like and adversarial in contrast to the perhaps intense but cerebral intrapsychic struggle in which parts of the self vie with one another and which is often experienced as a disturbing but familiar personal mini-drama. For all of these reasons, an interpersonal defense will carry with it a flavor of spontaneous danger that can not be present in the same way when the battlefield is pitched solely within the recesses of the individual psyche. Finally, in an intrapsychic defense such as obsessional thinking, there may be no expressive behavioral sign to signify an inner structural change is in the making; or such behavior may be considerably delayed; or, in the case of intrapsychic defenses such as denial or projection, behavior (which is especially directed towards another person) *may*, according to the interaction, follow. This is in sharp contrast to an interpersonal defense of the ilk of narcissistic giving which, by necessity, *must* terminate in manifest behavior.

So, while the basic strategy of narcissistic giving is to protect a fragile sense of an impaired capacity to relate in a nurturing way to another's needs, its enactment--being always within an interpersonal setting--will take some unusual although characteristic forms.

Here are some of the more significant ones:

DEPERSONALIZATION

Joe, a patient of mine, perceived himself to be in deep trouble. An intelligent but underachieving law student, he had been placed on probation and presented with the dilemma of either elevating his sagging grade average, in swift and dramatic fashion, or preparing himself for the ultimate academic disgrace of being summarily expelled from graduate school. Joe's initial panicky attempt at crisis self-management, in addition to entering therapy with me, was to enlist the services of Frank, the most highly prized tutor available.

In terms of our discussion of strategies of narcissistic giving, it is Joe's relationship with Frank that is most germane. For--being repeatedly struck by the depths of my patient's insecurity vis-a-vis his natural ability to integrate and assimilate the formidable mass of required juridical data and thought--I could not help but be curious as to how Frank, from an entirely different professional bias, would respond to his pupil's academic malaise.

Although I could envision (as I vicariously put myself in the shoes of Frank) a variety of plausible tutorial strategies by which to arrest Joe's demoralization, it did not occur to me there was another option: *not* to respond.

Yet, that is what transpired: Joe, each week anxiously dwelling on his fear of being unable to grasp a given fundamental point of law, and Frank--usually after offering some palliative such as "Sorry" or "Oh"--saying, "Let's get to the lesson, then."

What was startling to Joe (and revealing to me) was the almost eerie fashion in which Frank could, as though simply deaf to the insistent pleading of his pupil, adhere unruffled to his preplanned instructional outline: the degree of narcissistic giving being so extreme, that the issue was really not one of not having heard, but, perhaps, of never having adequately learned to acknowledge and to relate to another's needs.

Yet, being able to dissociate from a perceived obligation to respond in a minimally nurturing way--in this case to validate (if not alleviate) the serious impediment to academic progress created by acute performance anxiety--Frank was able to achieve a covert interpersonal aim: he could continue his depersonalized stance.

In this sense, depersonalization is an extreme strategy of narcissistic giving, generally employed by a person (such as Frank) who deep down is hopeless about the prospects of being able to meaningfully relate to someone else. A favorite tactic for maintaining a depersonalized stance is--as was the case with Frank--to transform what is plainly a request for emotional sustenance (Joe's plea that he be somehow benignly guided out of his morass of self-doubt) into a request for arid instruction (analogous to the previously mentioned trait of relating through information-giving).

When this occurs, it is not surprising that there is a disturbing disjunction between the person who is narcissistically giving and the one who is articulating, howsoever haltingly, some inner lack--so that it is yet one more characteristic of a narcissistic giving interaction that it never seems congruent. Which is not the same thing as saying it is non-reciprocal. A relationship can be non-reciprocal (e.g., a tutor and pupil) and yet be congruent inasmuch as both participants, albeit from different vantage points and disparate roles, are working collaboratively towards a mutual goal. By contrast, it is incongruent when, as in our example, a tutor chooses (unconsciously) to ignore a pupil's greatest problem (e.g., crippling performance anxiety) and yet behaves as though he were discharging his professional obligations in an exemplary fashion. Incongruity of this severity cannot be accidental: one of the defensive uses of the dissociation which is characteristic of depersonalization is to keep apart those things which in combination, would trigger anxiety; and someone such as Frank who relies upon dissociative distancing--should he suddenly become aware of the impairment of his capacity to be intimate signified by his depersonalization--would no doubt be suffused with anxiety. Much easier is it, as shown in the case of Frank, to be instead aware of a need to be precise, technical and, above all, unenthusiastic.

It is easy to castigate depersonalization as a relational pauper but, in our over-specialized and high tech society, there are many advantages to be gained from behaving in a depersonalized manner. First and foremost from our standpoint is that it allows one to justify sidestepping any demands to be more intimate on the grounds that such personalization is contextually inappropriate. This is because depersonalization generally carries with it the implicit message that not only are personal needs irrelevant to what is being transacted, but that they are intrusive. The implication clearly being that the connection which exists is certainly not a warm human one. It may be one of social convention, of necessity, of politeness, of informational exchange, but it is not one of feeling or of intimacy. Moreover, the stance of depersonalization seems to suggest that one is fully entitled to such reservation of one's feelings and such a holding in check of one's mood; and that the evident disinterest in being intimate with a fellow human being is in no way caused by a paralysis of the ability to relate or an ingrained aloofness, but is a reasoned and admirable choice.

Depersonalization, therefore, typically operates from a position of defensive, distancing superiority (because it has to) which sooner or later betrays itself by an intrusive condescension. Such condescension, however, is often felt to be necessary in order to shore up a precarious sense of self esteem and much of the strategy of the interpersonal defense of depersonalization is devoted to placing itself above, and safely beyond, the grasp of personalized relating. A variety of maneuvers are utilized to achieve this required comfort zone of interpersonal space. One is by inferring that whatever is at stake can best be approached by objectivity or resolved by objectivity and not subjectivity (i.e., it is the *wrong* strategy). Another is to devalue the status of subjectivity itself as something perhaps suspect or even weak. Yet another is to directly challenge the subjectivity of the other as being--not the honest articulation of the aroused self-- but a manipulative gambit to use the persuasive power of emotion to override the more temperate neutrality of reason so as to achieve an ulterior aim.

The latter is a fairly common paranoid reaction on the part of the depersonalized (and depersonalizing) person who sees the other's need to get closer as merely a covert counter-strategy by which to lull him into a dangerously false sense of security so as to be able (when necessary) to rob him of something. Closeness, from the perspective of the depersonalized stance, is either a threat, a pretense or a stratagem. Most often it is viewed as an irritation and disturbance in a kind of field of interpersonal detachment that the depersonalizing person is uneasily and, typically, frailly laboring to uphold. On the other hand, such depersonalization is rarely understood by its recipient who, in order to relieve some neediness, is usually striving to move within a position close enough to make contact and can, therefore, only regard the perceived reaction of obstinate pulling back as an intentional, painful rejection and not as the unconscious expression of an indiscriminate need for interpersonal withdrawal at any price.

The narcissistic giving component in the stance and strategy of depersonalization is now obvious: that by seeming to proffer measured distance, objective neutrality, a refusal to be provoked into tangential emotional exchanges or time-wasting pleasantries, one is giving something far more substantive than the satisfaction of someone's subjective need for personal closeness or warmth. From the vantage point of the stance of depersonalization, the satisfaction of intimacy needs represents a blatantly gratuitous gratification.

BEING OBJECTIVE

The attempt to relate by dispensing information (as my patient Max's older sister did) or by primarily focusing on the feelings of the other (in the manner of Charles) or through depersonalization, may be variously grouped under the broader heading of *trying to be objective*. Being objective, as an interpersonal strategy, implies: that one has entered into a mode where cognition is primary; where relationships are between ideas or qualities of things and not things per se (R.D Laing's "The objective look"); where the scientific method, logic and rational thought are considered indispensable to whatever project is at hand; and where results, bottom line and what is functional and utilitarian take precedence over what is spontaneously expressive, self-actualizing or self-validating. Furthermore, there is the injunction that processes of thought and categorizations of experience should have priority over simple experiencing (although there is also the implicit rationale that being objective--by allowing one to better shape the influx of raw perceptual stimuli--will eventuate in a textually richer state of mind).

What often happens instead, however, is that an insidious maneuver of withdrawing oneself from the realm of direct, meaningful experience is inaugurated which, over time, can lead to a kind of emotional detachment that bars one from the very goal for which is was originally set up. (One of the best descriptions of just how far-reaching and subversive this process can be, is given by R.D. Laing in *The Voice of Experience*. What Laing calls "the objective look" and "the diagnostic look", regarding them as symptoms of the western world's retreat from the primary data of experience, I, by contrast, treat as a simple but profound psychodynamic strategy for evading issues of intimacy.)

Entering the objective mode, therefore, implies that one is being objective by choice; guided by rational necessity and not by any subjective gratification in the act of being objective. Thus, being objective in interpersonal relations grants one the freedom to be impersonal or even, in extreme cases, depersonalized, yet, without having to take responsibility for one's subjectivity. Seen in this light, being objective used as a strategy of narcissistic giving, is always a highly subjective act. And since such subjectivity will typically be denied through the pretense of having transformed it into a more purified cognitive functioning--the presumed resultant objectivity cannot help but be contaminated by the disavowed but still operative, underlying subjectivity.

For that reason, it is often far more interesting to understand why people want to become objective than it is to learn whatever one is supposed to learn by attending to the process of their objectivity. Although the motives are myriad, in my experience people especially find it tempting to assume the mantle of objectivity when they are: in doubt; confused; frightened of feelings; or apprehensive that they are on the verge of being disconnected from another person. It is easy to see, when looked at from the standpoint of intimacy, that the interpersonal strategy of relating in an objective manner is notably lacking. That is because someone who is endeavoring to be objective, typically is not only not attempting to extend warmth, empathy or nurturance to someone else, but, as a consequence of the mandatory interpersonal neutrality, is prohibited from even trying. It is therefore enlightening to look at all the things one cannot do, if one is invested in acting objectively towards the other: one cannot directly express significant feelings; become committed to what one is saying; become enthusiastic; allow oneself to be in touch with one's ambivalence; give free reign to one's subjectivity; relax one's efforts to monitor or process one's mood; on occasion be temperamental, irascible, self-contradictory, playful, charming, sensuous or sexual (most of which makes us human in the ordinary sense, but all of which are interdicted by the simple self-command "be objective").

Viewed this way, the objective interpersonal relationship is a deprived relationship. However, since someone who relates objectively acts as though it were a choice, often for the good of the other, the implication is that he can return to the subjective mode of relating at will, once the task at hand is resolved. Thus, *the intimacy deprivation which is intrinsic to the interpersonal strategy of being objective is denied by pretending it is the outcome of an existential choice rather than the need-driven product of defensive fragility (which, as I believe, it more commonly is)*.

SHRINKING PEOPLE

As I have tried to show (especially in the area of "Just Business") narcissistic giving, as a strategy for eluding the complexities of intimate giving and relating, often contrives to reduce the issue or need at hand to a mere quest for concrete specifics. As though, for example, what is being requested is so simple that it can be met with a brute fact or a perfunctory action. It is therefore important to reiterate that it is impossible to ask for just a scrap of information and that there is no such thing as an isolated need that is not somehow embedded in the context of at least a rudimentary relationship. Thus, someone who inquires of a passerby as to what time it is, cannot do so without expecting that a certain implicit relationship be also validated: i.e., that the person requesting the time is not viewed as incompetent for not carrying a watch, but as someone understandably inconvenienced; that the person is not seen as someone in the habit of entreating strangers for assistance in the quotidian details of living and is therefore in no way to be judged socially or mentally inferior to the one of whom the correct time is being solicited.

This, by the way, was forcibly brought home to me by a patient, who, although quite intelligent and normally self-sufficient, had happened, in a depressed state and in an uncharacteristically pathetic voice to have asked for the time and had been shocked at the instant reply ("No") from a man who was visibly and indisputably wearing a watch. Unable to accept this indignity, my patient had glanced pointedly and accusingly at the other's watch and repeated his request. Suddenly, in a dawn of understanding, the man relayed the correct time, explaining, "I thought you said dime." To which my patient became far more mortified to think that someone had actually mistaken him for a beggar.

I can think of no request for even the most trivial piece of neutral information which does not also carry with it a parallel request that the dignity of the solicitor be granted. Another way of saying this is whenever two people interact, howsoever fleetingly and regardless of the impersonality of the transaction, a relationship is being defined which has needs of its own and which can therefore never be fully functional or utilitarian. As a rule of thumb, the needs of the relationship will be more complex (because unstated and always, to some extent, partially unconscious) and will therefore be more likely to go unsatisfied, creating tension and conflict. Now this is so, even when the interaction is relatively straightforward. When it is basically duplicitous, as is always the case when narcissistic giving is involved, the relationship need as such is more likely, or even guaranteed, to go unmet and to produce frustration. Which, in turn, is typically dismissed, producing more frustration. For all of these reasons, one of the prime strategies of narcissistic giving--of which focusing on concrete although tangential specifics (as described in "Just Business") is only a sub case--is to attempt to rid the encounter of most if not all of its dynamic, relational aspects by shrinking it to the simplest possible form. While there are a variety of ways to do this, all of them have the effect of exorcising intimacy. For example:

1. To deny meaningfulness to the transaction. Pretending that instead of a genuine need, there is only a request for information is a great way to do this.

2. To invalidate any claim that there is an underlying, non-verbal or serious emotional tone to the message being delivered.

3. And therefore (as a tactic for achieving one and two) to treat messages: non-contextually, just verbally, and, especially, as though they are primarily carriers of technical information.

To reduce a contextual relationship in this manner to an interchange and flow of information and to imply that whatever issue exists between two people is at bottom only a problem in information processing, is not just dehumanizing and humiliating, it is confusing and demoralizing. This is because it puts the other person immediately on the defensive, while subversively planting seeds of self-doubt. Is the human personal need of so little worth that it can be imperiously dispelled with a quick toss of an informational crumb? Crude as it may sound, in our increasingly high tech and information-overloaded society, it is a surprisingly easy and available strategy to employ, if one wishes to create emotional distance of any kind.

However, shrinking a human transaction to a question of information processing is merely one way of dehumanizing a relationship. Another is to stereotype it: that is, to isolate one or two components from the mosaic of characteristics which constitute a given individual and to emphasize these to the detriment of the others. While it is well known that stereotyping, by reducing complexity also reduces dignity, it is less often recognized that it is impossible for anyone, regardless of the level of their sophistication, not to stereotype or pigeonhole people some of the time. I suggest this is because stereotyping is related to gestalt perception and may be looked upon *as gestalt perception as applied to human personality*. Gestalt perception, it will be remembered, which grew out of an epistemological study of how perception arises, was founded on the discovery that there is not only an innate tendency for pattern recognition, but such a need for it, that it will impose premature closure (i.e., complete patterns or find patterns where there are none) in order to satisfy this perceptual craving.

In the realm of scientific theory-making, this kind of gestalt perception, if tempered by experimental verification, can be a potent tool because it can intuit potential or hidden patterns in a seeming welter of disparate sense impressions. In the realm of people recognition, however--unless one is a psychological genius of the calibre of, say, a Freud, Erik Erikson, R.D. Laing or W.R. Bion (and sometimes even in their cases, too)--gestalt perception inevitably leads one down the garden path of stereotyping. This is because in order to make sense of the influx of stimuli and to structure the mass of signals that will be exchanged between any two people in even a fragmentary encounter, there will be irresistible pressure to fall back upon pre-existing pattern recognition and categorization as explanatory reassurances. (Added to this is the fact that in contrast to the physical sciences, there is no ready means of experimental verification at hand to validate or invalidate such gestalt perceptions when applied to people.) And even if one were capable of the herculean task of taking a fresh look at every new moment of every personal transaction without prejudging it on the basis of past formulations, there would not possibly be enough time to do it. The result is the unhappy one of pigeonholing people into indiscriminate, and therefore demeaning, categories.

To return to the starting point of our discussion: when perceptions are prematurely formed in order to satisfy an apparent deep need for closure, we call this gestalt perception--when individuals are prematurely categorized in order to satisfy a similar need, we call this stereotyping. It becomes immediately apparent that it is far less destructive to impose premature closure on an impersonal perception, than it is to pigeonhole a human being.

Now the point is that while we all regularly stereotype one another (because we have to), that impulse is magnified and exploited in the case of narcissistic giving where there is a willful attempt to obliterate the status of the need for intimacy, by reductively dehumanizing the other.

This becomes clearer if we compare shrinking people with the kind of stereotyping that regularly takes place in the parallel world of advertising and marketing. To a certain extent both rely upon what the great ethologist, Konrad Lorenz, has called the Innate Releasing Mechanism (IRM). An IRM is a genetically programmed behavior pattern, constituted by a few basic behaviors (or a few principal behavioral strategies) which are triggered into dynamic play by the activation of a key stimulus (or releaser). While the degree of application of biological IRMs to human behavior continues to be hotly debated, what is important from our standpoint is that people often behave *as though they believed IRM's exist*. Nowhere is this more evident than in the practice of subliminal advertising where interpersonal relations, per se, are shrunk to almost cartoon proportions and yet, bizarrely, continue to exert a significant impact upon its audience. Seen this way, the gestalt perception or stereotype of the person would correspond to the IRM and certain salient ethnic characteristics--whatever supposedly makes a Jew perceived as a Jew, an Italian perceived as an Italian or an African-American perceived as an African-American--would correspond to the key stimulus (subliminal cue).

It is important to realize the kind of reductionism we are describing is not just a passive reliance upon preconceived stereotypes, but is the outcome of an active if unrewarding process. Although, traditionally, stereotyping has been regarded as a cognitive deficit, the product of a failure of education, here it is being looked at as something forged under the duress of facing a need to be genuinely and humanly giving which cannot be met, and yet cannot be postponed without sustaining an appreciable blow to one's self-esteem.

By now it should be clear there are numerous ways to shrink people. Adopting an interpersonal stance of being technically or informationally objective is one. Doing the reverse, however--acting towards the other in an emotionally primitive or infantile manner more appropriate to a child--is another. (In psychoanalysis such behavior, which is thought to be universal under certain conditions of stress and anxiety, is referred to as *transferential*: i.e., the regressive process by which a child-like imago of a perceived parental or authority figure derived from the past is erroneously mapped onto *or transferred to* an unrelated person in the present.) When such transferential reactions occur, whatever richness and complexity the adult person has, is reduced to a child's imago of what an interpersonal relationship is. It follows there is a substantial loss of mature objectivity. Yet, from the standpoint of shrinking, there is a telling similarity between the interpersonal posture of a superior objectivity (relating by attempting to be objective) and the childish reality distortion characteristic of so-called transferential reactions: i.e., in both there is a dramatic loss of the capacity to be maturely intimate.

We've already looked at some of the intimacy needs (for closeness, comfort, spontaneity, playfulness) that can be disposed of intrapsychically (within the person) through the simple expedient of trying to objective. Now let's look at some of the regular interpersonal needs that can be simultaneously dispensed with upon entering the objective mode. If one has frankly relinquished the obligation to be intimate with another because one is supposedly being objective, then there is no longer a requirement to respond to: manifest feelings of inadequacy; a need for contact; a need to be appreciated; a need to be understood; and a need to be granted the opportunity to understand as well--all of which in various degrees and permutations may be emanating from the other. On an even deeper level, it is no longer necessary to be concerned with the development of the other; with whatever conflict the other may be experiencing; with the appearance of signs of pain or the hint that what is really being asked for is something considerably more nourishing than the literal dissemination of technical information or impersonal judgment.

To relate, therefore, or more properly to avoid relating by striving to be objective--purely from the economical perspective of the psychical energy that might easily be expended in an interaction that could be characterized in any way as intimate--constitutes an enormous savings. And for this reason, it is unwittingly and pervasively reinforced in our cost-effective, high tech, computer-age culture, so that it not only routinely goes unchallenged, but it is almost totally unnoticed.

Such reductionism, especially when directed to the interpersonal sphere, fosters the illusion that it has now become feasible to control the reactions of the other, who, to that degree, is seen more as a puppet than a person and therefore more amenable to the technique of behavioral puppetry.

Other significant defensive uses of the narcissistic giving strategy of shrinking people therefore are:

1. To save energy through dispensing with the creative energy that is needed to deal with complexity (in this sense, being intimate equals the most complex interpersonal transaction while "being objective" equals the least complex).

The method of reductionism when applied to people, is uncreative because--unlike the pure scientist (e.g., Richard Feynman) who reduces the universe in order to abstract first principles and pristine theoretical models so as to more profoundly understand them--here there is no attempt to ultimately know the person in a deeper and more original way. Quite the contrary, the intent is--by utilizing so-called scientific objectivity in the most superficial and negative way (e.g., informationally)--to dismiss him.

2. To sponsor the illusion and false comfort that controlling people can somehow be a viable substitute for relating to people. It does this by contriving to view others as devoid of the need to relate and therefore more as automatons waiting or inviting someone to program them. In part, such a desire to control expresses itself interpersonally in the belief that what is at stake, what is necessary, is to repair some kind of utilitarian, functional or behavioral problem. But it is important to recognize that, underlying such aspirations to modify the behavior of the other, may be not so much a need to control as a *need not to be intimate* (so as, for example, to avoid being anxious).

3. To deliver the message that the holistic entity of the person, for whatever reason, cannot be respected--otherwise why the need for large scale reductionism? Shrinking implies, phenomenologically, that what you see is not what you get or is not enough, and that what is truly important is something else. Shrinking implies that the self as self is not worthy of being related to on its own terms and that what is necessary is an ad hoc self created (usually on the spot) to meet the needs of the dissatisfied other. In the eyes of the person being shrunk, of course, the process can feel like an eerie case of mistaken identity and that it must therefore be someone else whom the other has in mind. For this reason, a particularly demoralizing aspect of this type of strategy of narcissistic giving is that the self which the self takes itself to be bears almost no resemblance to the self as seen by the other.

Towards the end of the last chapter, I contrasted the relationship of entertainment based on immediate gratification with the type of relationship that is intended by authentic art. It was suggested that entertainment primarily anchored to the thrill of the now (e.g., soap opera) established a passive and even addictive relationship with its targeted audience and to that extent was gratifying in a narcissistic giving way, while mature, thoughtful art, representing as it did more developed and serious feelings, would set up a correspondingly more intimate relationship with its audience.

By intimate relationship with its audience I meant one which does not coddle and which strives for effects that depend largely on delayed gratification (because, being necessarily complex, they require sufficient time in which to be processed and assimilated). In this sense, a true work of art could be said to, first of all, *respect* its audience because, while giving a lot, it also asks for and expects a lot back (e.g., their rapt and patient attention over a considerable stretch of time) while simultaneously shunning the use of artistic devices designed to elicit premature, and therefore superficial, responses.

By contrast, what sales, marketing, advertising and narcissistic giving all have in common is a lack of respect for the autonomy of the person and a lack of trust in the ability of the person to give them whatever they want without attempting to, in effect, coerce it. Sales, advertising and narcissistic giving-- because they cannot conceive of someone independently choosing to satisfy their needs--all rely on immediacy of reaction: that is, they conspire, through overpowering the senses with selective stimulation or subliminal cues to, metaphorically and sometimes literally, take the money and run. Advertising is especially revealing in this regard and might be considered the business analogue of a narcissistic giving relationship; it focuses only on what it wants from the other (i.e., market) and everything it does is calculated to elicit a pre-determined, desired reaction. The narcissistic giving component in advertising, of course, is that none of this is acknowledged and that in its place is erected a highly stimulating, though hollow facade meant to convey the glittering message that something wonderful (indispensable and totally accessible product advantages) is being offered (to cover up the fact that the primary utilitarian intent is to give as little as possible while making the greatest feasible profit). Truly, both wish to break the bank: to invest a modest amount and to earn untold riches.

For all of these reasons, narcissistic giving--whether masking as entertainment, advertising, sales promotion, or interpersonal relating--will favor the strategy of shrinking people. If one will not or cannot respect others (if only because of excessive anxiety which drives one into self-absorption) trying to control them is an effective means of postponing the embarrassing realization that one is unable to relate. And trying to control the other always means seeing him or her as something emphatically less than someone who is existentially, humanistically and autonomously present.

SHRINKING STRATEGIES

1. The Cheerful Robot

One of the most efficient ways to shrink an interpersonal relationship, is by imposing an artificial cheeriness on a set of emotions that are anything but playful. To do so, is to opt for a premature closure by implying that things are running so smoothly that it is time to relax, to enjoy the moment and to even engage in some friendly horseplay. Someone who proclaims a state of well-being that does not seem to exist, or does not seem warranted by the known facts, can often succeed in thereby intimidating the other who may begin to feel that by refusing to accept the invitation to have fun he is somehow--regardless of the accuracy of his appraisal of the underlying mood of the occasion--being a spoilsport. Because it is surprisingly easy to do, people will try to control a situation by defining the emotional tone of it and they often do so as a defense against incipient anxiety. When an interaction between two people is emotionally defined in this way--from an arbitrary and unilateral perspective--it is typically intended to nip in the bud the development of any spontaneous, emotive interaction, flow or process. This type of stubborn, aggressive light-heartedness as a fail-safe response to almost every occasion is, of course, a well-known American relational characteristic. It is epitomized by the professional salesman, who has been trained to under no circumstances become discouraged or moody, but instead to be unwaveringly cheerful, if not ebullient, in the teeth of any rejection. Such mood control is by no means restricted to the salesman or to the random socializing of everyday life. It can flourish even in the objective mode, where it is not uncommon to see someone striving to be objective to the highest degree while simultaneously cultivating an attitude of unflagging good cheer: the implication being that one has for the present transcended the fluctuation and emotional turbulence of daily living and has marshalled a frolicsome abundance, an extra quota of energy and exuberance with which to invest in more mature and less self-absorbed pursuits.

2. The Denial of One's Intelligence and the Refinement of One's Obtuseness.

The other side of the coin of trying to act as though one is more objective than the other, is trying to act--when it suits one's purpose to do so--as though one is more obtuse. We are talking, of course, about willful obtuseness, which is commonly used as a defense against the interpersonal anxiety that is inevitably stirred up whenever one is invited to sharpen one's senses, set aside one's preconceptions and become receptive to the unknown experiential terrain of another human being. Examples are legion. Someone reveals in enthusiastic detail an idea one has been lovingly working on for months to a friend who seemingly listens attentively, and then offers absolutely no response. Or someone, who has been unhappy for a long time in a particular job and who finally elects to present a well-thought-out bill of grievances to a boss who is known for soliciting constructive criticisms, but who, on this crucial occasion, seems not only disinterested but positively bored. Or a lover, who upon being informed that he or she has been profoundly amiss when it comes to grasping what the other truly needs, simply chooses to ignore the remark. What all such instances have in common is a determination not to understand something that seems to cry out for understanding. Such misunderstanding cannot be accidental or innocent, and is based on unconscious denial. (Denial may be thought of as the result of an inability to differentiate and to relate to a specific threat: that is, to make sure that it dispels the offending, but unknown, irritant, it resorts to a global dismissal. It operates unconsciously in a similar fashion to the person who--spying a speck of dirt in a glass of water, but being uncertain as to how to purify a single speck--decides to throw the whole glass out. It is like a perceptual door which works like a material one: i.e., in order to shut out specific undesirables, it must initially exclude everyone. In other words, denial--so as to get rid of an indeterminate part--blindly rejects the whole).

When such denial comes into play between two people, it means that someone, at a certain point, will stubbornly put one's normal sensitivity and receptivity on hold. When being obtuse happens to be a characterological interpersonal defense then it generally connotes: that the person is only responding this way, because the other is not only not acting meaningfully, but has failed to achieve even comprehensible cohesiveness. Being defensively obtuse is a way of (unconsciously) trying to suppress what the other is saying and doing by subversively retarding one's receptivity and thereby slowing down the required reaction time. Such obtuseness, moreover, is almost always denied and safely projected onto the other: i.e., one does not comprehend, not because one is stupid, but because the other is not making sense. Being obtuse is a way of not having to go to the trouble of differentiating (one cannot be specific--and thereby take a risk--if one has not yet understood what is being said). It is a way of not having to respond, relate, emote, take a position and expose whatever it is one thinks and feels about what has just occurred. After all, you can't react to or make contact with what has yet to reach you.

In this sense, being obtuse changes passive to active and effectively turns the tables on the other, who is held responsible for not making a sufficiently meaningful impact on the listener. Thus, it is the *other* who must respond better and do more in order to get the transaction jump-started and not the puzzled recipient who cannot help but appear obtuse.

There is a distinction, it should be noted, between the narcissistic giving strategy of being defensively obtuse and that of the previously mentioned withholding personality ("Waiting For Godot"). The difference being that the withholding personality, far from behaving as though it has failed to comprehend, acts as though it understands all too well what has been said and done--but that it is *beneath* its consideration. So, while the defensively obtuse person seems to suggest that he will reply once he understands, the withholding personality implies that it will react only on the condition of hearing something meritorious.

Seen this way, they are two sides of the same coin and the narcissistic giving component in both should be obvious: the withholding personality comports itself as though its allegiance to a higher standard of communication and refusal to be dragged down to a relationship based on trivia, is somehow a contribution to a potentially better interaction and therein a gift to the other who is annoyingly lagging behind; while the strategically obtuse person, by forthrightly showing his bafflement, is thereby giving the other some invaluable corrective feedback on his deficiency in communicating.

3.   Reductionism

The various means by which human transactions are denuded of their intimacy needs all depend, in one way or another, on a philosophy of reductionism. This does not mean, however, that reductionism per se is bad. In point of fact there are several types. One, of course, is the much-denounced practice of indiscriminate and therefore irresponsible reductionism attributed to tunnel-vision scientists. On the other end of the continuum, however, is the reductionism of a bona fide creative genius such as the great particle physicist, Richard Feynman, who, as already alluded to, wanted to reduce intricate phenomena of nature down to first principles, not for the pleasure of deconstructing, but in order to better understand how to *construct* complexity (build it up from elemental units). In his wonderful biography of the legendary scientist, James Gleick shows, over and over again, the almost magical joy Feynman derived from his ability to take pristine principles of nature and use them as though they were a child's building blocks. As its best, as was certainly the case with Richard Feynman, reductionism can be thought of as creativity, but *going in a different direction*; it goes backwards (reduces) only in order to triumphantly march forward. Because of that, it never abandons, never loses sight of what it is reducing. It does this by balancing the fleshed-out, quality-rich world on the one hand with the theoretically reduced, toy-model version on the other hand. Far from deconstructing the world because he has lost interest in it, the true scientist simply steps back so as to reapproach it with a fuller and deeper understanding. In his hands, not only is there no desire to shrink, devalue or diminish the known universe, but there is a passionate yearning to, in an abstract way, form a more intimate relationship with it. A creative genius such as Richard Feynman seems urgently to want to make the universe known to him, since obviously he can not make himself known to the universe. It might therefore be said that this type of ardent reductionism is an attempt at reparation to the self for the lonely truth that this relationship must forever be non-reciprocal and, especially, *non-intimate*: i.e., you (the world) can never know me--so I must compensate by not only knowing you better, but by being able to manipulate and creatively synthesize you. (In this instance, scientific reductionism can be viewed as theoretical regression in the service of the creatively synthesizing ego.)

Now, let's look at its antithesis, non-creative and dehumanizing reductionism, the strategy preferred by interactions we have characterized as narcissistically giving. One way to understand this, is to understand what it is *not*--that is, to take note of everything which gets left out or thrown out in the process of reducing people. If we do that, we see that such psychical subtraction pertains to certain fundamental attributes without which it would be difficult to maintain the designation human being: e.g., imagination, thought, qualities, meaning, consciousness, experience and emotion. Furthermore, it becomes immediately apparent that the more of these fundamental attributes which are deleted, the more we tend to label the transformation reductive in the pejorative sense.

It is important, therefore, that science, especially the queen of physical sciences, physics, does not address any of these attributes. (Richard Feynman, himself, in one of his more philosophical musings which delighted so many people, pointed out that all of the master equations of modern physics are alike in that they do not contain qualities: "What we really cannot do is deal with the actual, wet water running through a pipe. That is the central problem which we ought to solve some day"--and he openly expressed the fond hope that perhaps one day qualities, such as real flowing water, might find a place in the equations).

Although it is perhaps this very omission that holds the key to the spectacular reductive success of modern physics, it is nevertheless true and has long been known that the process of creativity--involving as it does thoughts, reveries, dreams, memories, subjective wishes, fantasies--is essentially no different inside the hard sciences than it is outside them. What is less understood and therefore not sufficiently appreciated is that in an enterprise such as physics the product of creativity is almost exactly similar to both the procedure for reducing it and to the method for experimentally verifying it. In other words, whatever result you get, it is always something that can be measured and quantified, and since the method of verifying the validity of such reductionism just happens to work only on objects that are measurable and quantifiable, you might way that there is a prearranged and even collusive harmony.

Nothing of the sort exists in the so-called life sciences (e.g., psychoanalysis) where the product of the creative process (e.g., a psychodynamic theory about the unconscious meaning of behavior) bears little resemblance and seems hardly compatible with the rigorous reductionism of the physical sciences. This, of course, is because psychodynamic theories of human behavior of necessity, and to various degrees, contain attributes of thought, quality, meaning, experience, imagination and emotion. Which in turn means that if one wishes to weed out these very same attributes (so as to conform to the preferred model of physical science) then one must first radically transform and operationalize the subject matter of the nascent theory at hand in order for it to become grist for the reductive mill.

It now becomes clear that physical science, beginning as it does with a perfectly suitable object to investigate--one that intentionally is measurable and quantifiable--needs no such alteration and therein contains a huge advantage over the life sciences regarding its prospects for success. This is why life sciences which strive to emulate the reductive models of physics--e.g., statistical social science, experimental psychology and, especially, behaviorism--strike so many people as offensively dehumanizing. Yes, they are measuring something. But what? At what cost, and is it significantly human?

A simple chessboard analogy may clarify why reductionism in physical science makes so much more sense than in the life sciences. When chess is played at the level of a Bobby Fischer, then the product of such creative genius (whose process may be tempestuous, intuitive and willful)--by being only pieces of wood aligned in geometrical positions on a material board--is immediately accessible to instant verification (in terms of whether it is a winning or losing position). What this means is that whatever tactical mistakes have been unconsciously committed, can at once be spotted and subsequently discarded. No such luxury of almost instantaneous corrective feedback exists in the life sciences and should even a Bobby Fischer direct his creative genius towards the construction of a reductive model of human behavior comparable in elegance to a strategic position on the chessboard, it would become clear how swiftly the odds would shift against the success of such an enterprise.

From this standpoint, it is easy to see why the most successful explanatory model for human beings in this century has probably been behaviorism: because it deliberately leaves out of its formulations thought, quality, meaning, imagination, experience and emotion. Yet, for the very reason that it so effectively dehumanizes people (whether it does so intentionally or unwittingly, by its altruistic allegiance to impartial science) behaviorism is a favorite reductive strategy of narcissistic giving. This means that transactions that can be so characterized invariably feature one person imagining or treating the other as a less-than-human stereotypical figure: only a discernible chain of crude causes and motives terminating in obvious and easy-to-manipulate behavior.

All strategies of narcissistic giving are therefore shrinking strategies and have this in common: they find it more expedient--rather than to try to contain or relate to the core intimacy needs of the self and the other--to purge them.

CHAPTER THREE

The Mirror Up To Nature

ART AS SEDUCTION

If, as I believe, narcissistic giving, to a profound degree, passes for genuine relating in nearly every sector of contemporary life, then surely we must repeatedly glimpse its image in the reflecting mirrors of art. In order to locate and delineate such an image more precisely, I have characterized essentially two different kinds of artistic mediums: one that forms a relationship with its audience that may be described as narcissistic giving and one that--spurning shortcuts and manipulations that are increasingly available--honestly endeavors to establish a more meaningful, enduring and intimate bond.

Let me therefore briefly summarize the points already made: Narcissistic-giving art, inasmuch as it has no intention of developing an in-depth relationship, channels its energies instead toward manipulating, titillating and seducing and, since there is no desire to make contact, other than immediacy of effect, there is neither a need to be known by nor a need to truly know its audience. In this sense narcissistic-giving art is that of the quick score, the first strike and the philosophy of take the money and run. By contrast, art that wishes to speak more intimately to its imagined audience will aspire to a more durable if abstract relationship. Although it will go to exhaustive lengths in order to make itself known, it will also be unafraid to demand of its audience the serious investment of time and effort that may be necessary to truly comprehend its complexity. (The classic example being the mind-boggling concentration that is required to even have a clue as to what is going on in Joyce's masterpiece, *Ulysses*.)

In the present chapter, I would like to develop these ideas in greater detail. My focus here, as elsewhere in the book--since my primary purpose is to demonstrate both the range and the ramifications of the interactional phenomenon I call narcissistic giving--will be on *relationship*. While I am cognizant of the many differences between a symbolic, aesthetic relationship, such as that constituted by an artist or art form and its audience, and one that is interpersonally lived in the ordinary sense of the term--it is to the *similarities* that I wish to address myself. And that is because I view the peculiar bond which exists between art form and audience as sufficiently symbolic of the less grandiose, more commonplace transaction between everyday people to merit its own special consideration. It should be noted, for the purpose of this discussion, that what has been termed either pop art or commercial art (which probably accounts for the lion's share of what passes for artistic fare in this country) will be lumped together, herein to be referred to as narcissistic-giving art.

Now, once narcissistic-giving art is taken seriously and looked upon as an embodiment (admittedly abstract and aesthetic) of a kind of interpersonal relationship between an artistic medium and its audience, then certain salient characteristics that have been described in simple one-on-one encounters immediately become apparent. Perhaps foremost is that narcissistic-giving art relies heavily on an assortment of techniques that have one thing in common: they are blatantly seductive. As an interpersonal encounter and process between two people, seduction may be said to be something which has no process. By that I mean at the heart of the seductive project is a concerted effort, by whatever means available, to convince the other that there is no longer a need to delay gratification because, in effect, you can have it without working for it. In this regard, the strategy of seduction, like the technique of narcissistic-giving art, is similar: it tries to corrupt by strongly suggesting that, vis-a-vis the payoff that is being dangled, time and process (which are intrinsic components in intimate relationships and in intimate art) are in this instance gratuitous constraints because immediate thrills are manifestly available. Someone who wishes to seduce another--whether into premature emotional or sexual compliance--operates on the principle that if he or she can skillfully demonstrate that a decided but safe shortcut to an intensely pleasurable gratification is at hand, then sooner or later it will prove irresistible. The unconscious interactive model being used here, of course, is derived from the effects of fast-acting drugs and, curiously, from the principles of behaviorism and behavior modification which essentially teach that only behavior which is immediately and consistently rewarded will be reinforced (thereby automatically ruling out the long-term, complex, unpredictable and delayed gratification that is so characteristic of intimacy and intimate art).

Like all seduction, narcissistic-giving art is inherently subversive: it actively subscribes to the cynical but widespread contemporary belief (which unfortunately gains considerable physiological support from the demonstrated mechanisms of addictive drugs) that the psyche will not be able to, or the human nervous system is unable to, resist a concentrated and immediate assault on its respective pleasure centers (whether psychological or endorphin-based). Or to put it another way: once you can begin to soften up the person's natural resistance to shallow self-indulgence by subversively stimulating those primitive pleasure centers of the brain and its psyche with fast-acting positive reinforcements--you will effectively make it harder and harder for him or her to sustain the required motivation for the long-range satisfaction of intimacy and of intimate art. If this is so and narcissistic-giving art is unashamedly, seductively subversive, the question arises--what basically does it aspire to subvert? (The answer must be: any hope or belief that one can establish an intimate relationship with either another person or with a symbolically meaningful artistic proxy).

A second important characteristic that has also been described in simple one-on-one encounters, is the paucity of communication. It is a hallmark of someone who is initiating a narcissistic-giving transaction that his behavior--other than possible reactions to the perceived success or failure of his interpersonal maneuvering--will tell you almost nothing as to what he is really thinking or feeling. That is because enactments of behavioral strategies, whether in business, in chess matches or in an entertainment field predicated upon techniques of manipulation, are constituted so as to provide no useful information about the underlying personal relationship. Unlike a true work of art which at some point, howsoever circuitously or symbolically, is driven to reveal its deepest meaning so as to be known, what we call narcissistic-giving art is bent only on the perfection of its strategy of audience-gratification. Accordingly, someone who chooses to be a spectator to a typical product of such a strategy (e.g., a daytime soap opera) will not have a clue as to the possible real identity of the author of the particular show he is watching (because, intentionally, no such clue was given).

FAME

Narcissistic-giving art is synonymous, in this country, with being popular art, but it is a popularity of such awesome proportions that it comes much closer to what we commonly refer to as fame: that is, we have protagonists who are famous, caught up in equally famous melodramatic conflicts, who either sing famous songs, participate in celebrated car chases, engage in ritualized sexual practices or acts of violence guaranteed to elicit levels of audience arousal so well-documented that they too have become famous. All this is so familiar and taken for granted that what is often overlooked is the essential role the state of being famous plays in the actual dynamics of artist-audience interaction. While the *effects* of such fame are exhaustively tabulated by market research specialists, and while the determinants and putative *causes* of such fame are even more faithfully studied by public relations experts and entertainment industry analysts in the hope of learning how to emulate and to therefore manipulate them--very little attention is paid to the *experience* or phenomenology of fame from the interpersonal standpoint of being an actual relationship.

Part of the reason for this, of course, is that, from the vantage point of the ordinary person, fame is perhaps the most distal, yet vivid relationship conceivable. It is that unique circumstance in which someone perceives himself or herself to be bonded, committed and even intimate with an other whom one has never known. It is barely described, and only superficially explained by the designation "fan". It is, instead, a rare interpersonal event and it may be said to arise when: the impact of the person who subsequently becomes famous is so extraordinary that it *can be internalized without the necessity of ever being corporeally present.* When one thinks about it, there is no greater testimony to the impression that a solitary person can have on an extended group. There is no other example in which an individual can exert a meaningful psychological force on the other without even having to bother to show up. Because all other instances of perceived interpersonal impact require, at one time or another, at least minimal presence, being famous can seem, in a mysterious way, to be somehow the result of an extra-sensory extension and psychical ripple effect of a far-away, and magical person.

While to the unique individual who acquires it, fame itself can become another kind of interpersonal relationship, albeit extraordinary, that over time, becomes internalized--to the average person (who is forever denied the continuity of experience necessary to incorporate it) fame will be regarded as an exclusively external phenomenon.

Because it is so foreign to everyday human affairs, the experience of becoming famous, even in an illusory scaled-down way--that is, by listening to one's voice recorded for the first time on tape or viewing oneself making one's debut on a home video--is typically uncomfortable and somewhat disorienting. One of the reasons for the frequent initial jolt is the automatic resistance our psyches put up to being forced to perceive ourselves the way others perceive us and not the way our superegos do, or want to. In this regard, the experience of listening to oneself on tape or watching oneself on film can be not unlike having one's superego externalized and captured by an anonymous audience. Because a record or film can operate on the basic flux of experience in a way no human being can duplicate--by freezing it--it offers a rare opportunity to be a voyeur of one's self. Hearing one's voice or witnessing how one's face and body express itself through time allows one to observe that which was never seen or heard before. By so intensifying and purifying the self's experience of the self, it *alters* it. Listening to oneself or viewing oneself in this way is akin to watching a favorite movie a second time around: all the energy that was previously caught up in the suspense of not knowing how the pivotal plot will turn out, is suddenly free to explore the subtler and more muted details of what actually happened. Similarly, a recording or a film of the self allows one to focus in a far more exclusive and concentrated manner than was possible when one was naturally preoccupied (the first time around) with the outcome of whatever one was saying or doing as well as with the outcome of what proximate others were saying or doing.

But freezing the experience of the self means also preserving it and a nasty side effect can be the weakening of repressive tendencies that were originally called into play in order to uphold the image of oneself one wanted. Analogous to how attention is greatly narrowed this second time around--as one listens to and watches oneself--the operation of repressive tendencies is now restricted to only the *aftermath* of those images and sounds of sensuous reality it once actively worked on: that is, to possibly the emotional reactions and fresh interpretations afforded by this retrospective view of oneself, but *not* to the pristine experience itself. For this reason, a record or film of the self can tend to undermine past repressions and to act as an antidote to present ones, and therein be a bit of a shock to the psyche.

It is not surprising. To retrospectively encounter oneself memorialized on record or film this way is equivalent *to the experience of experiencing a self experience converted into a public experience.* It is a radical and sudden transformation, seemingly devoid of the slightest process, a kind of quantum jump from one image of the self to another, for which people are generally unprepared.

It is no less a shock, when a public self is suddenly and dramatically shrunken to a private one, as can occur when the customary anonymity of strangers is shattered by the chance encounter with a truly famous person. It is not uncommon at least once in a lifetime, or several times if you live in a city such as New York, to be walking down the street and to find yourself not more than a few feet from a body and face which until then had dwelled exclusively within the privileged domain of the motion picture screen or the family television set. The jolt of meeting someone famous for the first time is the jolt of having a familiar fantasy sector of experience abruptly collapse and of being simultaneously forced, whether one wants to or not, to reconstruct starting from scratch a new and strangely uncomfortable image of the other. That is because up close the person who heretofore had existed only as a magnification and creation of the media will necessarily appear to be in the flesh either taller or shorter than one had imagined, fatter or thinner, younger or older, handsomer or uglier, more humane, friendlier, kinder, more interesting-looking, or, less so--but *never the same.* The difference will be as fundamental as that between reality and imagination, between fact and fantasy. What this means is that someone who unexpectedly encounters a famous other--an other perhaps long held in high esteem and with whom one may have engaged in numerous imaginary but intense interactions--is also faced with the realization that a nexus of familiar fantasy experiences, whether prized or not, has just expired, a nexus which if not to be mourned, must at least be replaced. (I am aware of, and in no way want to discount the occasional *mania* which can seize a person upon meeting in the flesh a favorite hero or heroine.)

If we switch the perspective one more time, to the vantage point of the famous person, to whom every stranger is a potential fan, the type of interpersonal relationship that comes into play is even more curious, if only because it is a regular occurrence. As a therapist, who has spent many years working with struggling young artists who have come to New York City in order to realize their dreams of reaching stardom, I have sometimes had the rare opportunity of being privy to the process by which someone becomes actually famous. Although it is customary to chronicle the extraordinary privileges, as well as the tragedies, that can follow in the wake of having one's persona exponentially elevated by the media, it is less appreciated how stressful it is to be required to uphold the identity of fame with everyone you meet.

Here are some other oddities to be dealt with, that accompany the process of becoming famous:

1. Your normal private self image, prior to becoming known, must be transformed in a way that makes sense, so as to incorporate the public objectivication of you that is rapidly taking place. This is tantamount to being obliged, on short notice, to assemble a new identity.

2. People regularly know you, whom you don't know, something which never occurred before. While on the one hand this may feel like a gratifying extension of the boundaries of your presence, on the other hand, it can seem like an unwanted and unavoidably risky exposure to perhaps unseen enemies. Part of the task of internalizing the new relationship of being someone who has just become famous, therefore, means adjusting to the heightened paranoid fears that are an inevitable offshoot of the abnormal exposure to numerous people who could have you at a disadvantage if they were so inclined.

3. Your adjustment must also include handling the increased pressure and stimulation arising from the almost unlimited opportunity to be as pathologically grandiose as you wish.

4. Survivor's guilt must be dealt with, not only to your closest family and friends, but to the overwhelming mass of seemingly good people who will never reach the heights you have.

5. It has to be accepted that the relationships you can look forward to will be predominantly non-reciprocal. However, there are benefits to this peculiar interpersonal arrangement: i.e., normally nothing is required outside of your presence in order to fulfill the needs of the other. It is therefore incredibly easy when you are famous to please people: all you have to do is acknowledge the fact, as they approach, that they are not

merely units from an anonymous crowd but do indeed have an independent existence. By the same token, it is easy to appear to be generous--by rescuing them from their existential limbo--and to thereby make them grateful. (The fan whose existence is so validated, in a sense becomes famous, too: the primitive logic being that if the person who is most unknown to you and most famous to you is suddenly taking the time to know you, then it may be that something in you worthy of becoming famous which you never noticed is attracting the one who has already achieved it. It can then seem to the enraptured fan who has met a celebrity, that, in a process akin to contiguous magic, by being linked to fame, he has acquired it. And there can arise the unconscious syllogism: all of this person's experience is famous; I am now part of this person's experience; therefore, I, too, am famous.)

6. Finally, being famous is also a way of becoming charismatic, even if you are not, because fame carries with it its own brand of charisma. It differs from the traditional charismatic personality which typically showcases its ability to dramatically externalize and to project onto others its innermost psychical world. By contrast, most of the charismatic power of the person who is famous is derived second hand from observing its impact on the public: the fact that an anonymous mass of unconnected people, which normally is indifferent or even hostile to strangers, can enthusiastically respond to an *unseen presence*, by inference, can conjure up an image of a faraway potent force (the behind-the-scenes charisma of the one who is eliciting the fame-response). When, however, in the company of a truly charismatic individual--although, certainly, an awareness of the impact on the people around you will magnify your response--the focus is mainly on the charismatic person himself and the almost magical way he can seem to be broadcasting his psyche; whereas, in the case of fame, the reverse is true and the emphasis is on the wondrous impression that a seemingly ethereal presence can have on innumerable people. And since people respond so much more excitedly to someone who is celebrated from afar than to those who dwell in comparative anonymity in the immediate here and now, it can seem that the life force animating a distant famous person must be proportionately greater.

To sum up, *the state of being famous is the most powerful illustration and evidence of the charismatic impact that a solitary individual can have on a widespread and undifferentiated group of people.* When this kind of potency is joined to the ability to manifestly broadcast one's inner world--as it is in the successful performing artist--you have someone who combines the best of both worlds: the charisma of the person who can project himself or herself, right before your eyes, to an anonymous crowd and the secondary vicarious charisma which seems to emanate like a mysterious wave from the manifestly mesmerized audience.

BOBBY BECOMES A STAR

A clinical vignette of someone who--to his amazement and to mine-- actually became famous can perhaps bring the process to life. The first thing I would like to note, and what still lingers years after the occurrence, was the element of *surprise*. Although it is commonplace for ambitious young artists to not only dream but to endlessly scheme in their unabashed goal of attaining fame and glory, it is all too sadly true that they almost never succeed in devising or in stumbling upon a formula that really works. Far more likely is it, that a series of happy accidents begins to illuminate a certain avenue of artistic expression that, for a variety of idiosyncratic and largely mysterious reasons, proves to be unusually propitious.

And in retrospect, as both Bobby and I agree, that is exactly what happened to him. When he first came to see me, the idea of becoming famous was perhaps the furthest thing from his mind. At age forty--an especially traumatic one for an unemployed and by now thoroughly exhausted artist--he had more pragmatic things in mind: how, for example, to make peace with his passionately involved, but deeply disappointed and forever demanding wife; how to continue to rationalize working as a freelance musician when, over the past ten years, he had never earned more than five thousand dollars from his music in a single year; and, perhaps most unnerving, how could he ever accept the dreary prospect, which was being economically forced upon him, of returning to the financial mainstay of his youth, the job that he despised--being a waiter.

This was the kind of impasse--that I know all too well--which drives young artists, and artists who were once young, as a last resort into the offices of therapists. From experience, I have learned not to try to do the impossible: which means, I leave the practical realization of their dreams of glory to themselves, or to others. I focus instead on the art of the possible, which in their case means taking up again real-world issues that have been left by the wayside in their haste to pursue their solitary vision. It also means, however, that I take seriously the terrible import they attribute to their inner world; and that I recognize that perhaps nothing is so vital to their eventual peace of mind as finding a way to create a meaningful bridge, that is, one that is real, between the two worlds which every artist inhabits.

So, in that first, year, Bobby and I spoke of many things: his failing marriage which he did not seem to know how to repair, try as he might; his disappointment over his inability to earn, after many years, a decent living; his cynicism as to his chances of ever being artistically validated, let alone discovered; his confusion as to how best to define his needs, to assert them, and, especially, to stand behind them; and, perhaps most poignant, his lingering sense of being an involuntary isolate, someone who longed for but could not make effective contact with the world about him.

Although progress was gradual, as it usually is, the work we did together-- as I appraised it and experienced it--flowed. Bobby was neither unpleasant, nor trying to be with. If anything, he was on the delightful side. He had a whimsical sense of humor, a flair for language which I appreciated, and a way of putting his own highly original take on everything he perceived, that I found fascinating. The therapeutic rapport between us, I felt confident, was both genuine and easy.

When he invited me to listen to a tape of what he personally considered his most creative musical composition, I was naturally curious. While I know that it is virtually impossible for a therapist to predict what kind of validation of artistic worth the world has in store for a particular patient-artist, and although I am scarcely a musician, I nevertheless do trust my artistic sensibility. I therefore felt I had a reasonable chance of intuiting, through the medium of music, something I did not know about Bobby, something which might be important from the standpoint of therapy.

So I listened to the tape, several times, in the privacy of my home. What I heard seemed strange, haunting, and certainly beautiful. A kind of atonal unfinished symphony, existing on many levels, going at numerous tempos, joining and then separating various disparate and sometimes almost floating sounds. It did not sound like anything I had heard before. Although I had been cautioned beforehand that what I would hear was not meant for commercial consumption, I realized that for about ten years Bobby had struggled to convince himself that the creation of such music was the chief justification for an existence that offered few rewards and often came perilously close to being unbearable. A great deal was at stake, therefore, and it seemed to Bobby that if there were to be any hope at all for him in this world, it would come from the hands of that artistic soulmate who would at long last appreciate, accept and above all, publish his unique music.

At that very time neither Bobby nor I had the slightest clue that he was on the cusp of a process that in a comparatively short time would send him zooming to stardom. When it came, interestingly enough, it had nothing whatsoever to do with his serious music. If anything it had to do with a talent he possessed, a talent for which he personally had no respect: he could write jingles.

Because of that, years ago, a little known photographer, who would later himself become famous--who had once heard one of those jingles and liked it--had paid Bobby a very small sum of money for permission to use the tune as background music for an industrial he had been working on at the time. Back then, Bobby had been only too happy to accommodate. After all, they were fellow artists, both poor, both struggling.

But now, seven years later, the photographer who by this time had become a very famous man in the world of advertising, had returned with a very different proposition. This time he was working on a commercial, one with a gigantic musical budget and it had seemed to him that the right man to do the music was Bobby. Would he consider whipping up a demonstration musical score, on speculation, of course, that he could present to the advertising agency executives who were in charge?

Working "on spec", as Bobby pointed out to me, was a euphemism for working for nothing. The supposed benefit, if he should agreed, would be a promissory one: if the demonstration ad was approved, it might go on national TV; if it went on national TV, Bobby's musical background score might get noticed; if it got noticed, it might lead to substantial remunerations. Although well aware of this potential, and mindful of the fact he could ill afford to let any opportunity slip by, he also knew--after ten years of practically giving himself away, artistically--that he could no longer tolerate working for nothing.

So Bobby, for the first time, took a stand: he calculated what he considered to be the rock bottom fee he would accept for the job that had been proposed to him and he resolved that he would refuse to work for a penny less. When the photographer, a few days afterwards, invited him out to dinner--in order to consummate the deal--Bobby wasted no time in announcing that the sum of fifteen hundred dollars, was "only fair" for the work that would be involved. To his surprise, and unmitigated delight, the famous photographer, without blinking an eye, said, "Sure."

At age forty, and after ten years of peddling his wares, that was the most money Bobby had ever earned for a single job. More importantly, it represented step one in his ascent to the top. Step two came five weeks later when the photographer contacted him again with a similar proposition, although this time he was careful to include a concrete offer of money.

Over the next few months, other gratifying offers of money to write musical background for industrials, TV or radio commercials slowly materialized. At first there did not seem to be any pattern to them, the only common denominator being that Bobby was now working more steadily and making more money than he ever had. And since he had never put much stock in being a commercial artist--it had never been his dream--he did not, initially, pay too much attention to the attention that people were beginning to pay him.

But it is in the nature of the process leading to fame that there is a critical point, after which the pace becomes so abnormally accelerated that it seems nothing can stop it. For Bobby that critical point came when an old friend--who had managed to gather the necessary capital to do his first feature film--unexpectedly asked him to write the entire musical score for the picture.

That was the first great surprise. Although the idea was appealing, Bobby had never envisioned writing background music for a film and he had no way of knowing whether he could measure up to even modest expectations. But he discovered, to his delight, that he could do it--not only easily, but exceptionally well.

Word travelled quickly through the advertising agencies of this extra dimension to Bobby's talent and it now seemed appropriate that such a man--far from being asked to work for as little as possible--should be richly rewarded for his time and effort. So offers that had been fifteen hundred dollars swelled to three thousand dollars and then six thousand and then ten thousand.

There was one memorable session when Bobby, who looked especially tired, explained that he had arisen earlier than usual in order to meet an important deadline. He had arranged, just prior to the session, to make a presentation to a board of advertising executives of some musical ideas, to be used as a theme for a multi-national company that grossed in the billions. If accepted, the theme would be played incessantly on national television and radio and Bobby would stand to make a fortune. When I could not resist asking how he had prepared for such a career-making job, he replied, "I didn't prepare. I just took an old song I had written when I was sixteen years old. I knew it was perfect for them, as soon as they told me what they wanted."

What was even more astonishing than the fact that he had been right--as one the board of executives had risen to their feet at the end of his presentation and given him a standing ovation--was the almost magical confidence he now clearly had in his own ability. It was as though a door had opened and Bobby had discovered that in the realm of music at least he could do anything he wanted: he could write jingles, background music for national TV ads, musical scores for motion pictures, atonal symphonies.

Nor did he think his talent or creativity at age forty any better than it was at age thirty or at any point during the preceding ten years when he had been teetering on the brink of poverty. But something had happened: he had learned, somehow, that he could take a stand. In the process he had found a connecting path, a bridge, between his idiosyncratic inner world and the mundane one he shared in common with everyone else. To his great surprise, he realized that simply by bringing forth his personal riches and boldly displaying them he could be rewarded beyond his fondest and most boyish dreams.

Although less than one artist in a hundred can ever expect to financially support himself while developing his craft, and much less than one artist in a thousand can ever plausibly hope to become what is called a star, in those rare cases where I have been able to document a rise to legitimate stardom, the dynamics of fame have been surprisingly consistent.

My focus here as elsewhere is on the nature of the interpersonal relationship that is fostered by the state of being famous. One way to understand that is to look at the *changes* that are incurred as one is drawn ever more deeply into the process of becoming publicly known.

Some of the most fundamental changes that then come to light--as seen in the case of Bobby and others--are:

1. The common apprehension of waiting for the other shoe to drop. While there is a sense of unreality permeating the entire process of

becoming famous, it is especially hard to adjust to the existential novelty that one can no longer count on being anonymous to the stranger one meets. (What then becomes clear is how much basic ontological anonymity can function as a *defense*.)

2. The need to deal with both the fear of and the desire to sabotage one's unbelievable, new found success. In addition, one must contend with the daunting perception that one has moved to a level of competitiveness never before experienced: if only because the number of people who would like to compete with you has vastly increased. (Perhaps nowhere is this more evident than in big time professional sports where the more you win, and the more you earn, the more likely you are to become a designated target of the competitive and organized greed of others.)

3. A sense that the tables have been turned and that instead of pursuing, one can afford the luxury at long last of pausing and waiting, of allowing oneself even to be pursued for a change, because, in effect, the chase is over. This is why a common characteristic of someone who is famous, at least in his or her public persona, is that of being supremely *unhurried*: compared to everyone else who seems restless or in motion, the famous person appears at rest--as though there is all the time in the world to accomplish what needs to be done, or that what has to be done, has already been taken of.

To a certain extent, the one who is famous is like a conductor of an orchestra, someone whose function it is to set the theme in motion and before whom others wait to be directed. Thus, typically, when such a person appears, there is a hush: if someone then poses a prodding or deferential question, there is a second hush, to see the direction in which the question will be taken (and the audience with it).

Psychic energy tends therefore to radiate in only one direction: from the rare person outward, and because this literally is never observed to happen in human affairs--a single person's presence having the uncanny ability to almost instantaneously suppress and bring to a halt the incessant interpersonal interactions that characterize regular public life--the famous individual is viewed as a kind of psychic freak: someone who can actually if only momentarily integrate a host of until then disparate, and predominantly solitary selves. From this vantage point, such an individual may begin to resemble a superhuman ego, an organizing force that far transcends the known boundaries, the real or imagined experience of ordinary people. And the power to impose such sudden order is especially impressive inasmuch as the one who is famous does not appear to be doing anything other than simply being.

4. The acquisition of fame is so discontinuous as to be akin to a quantum jump. Because of this, its arrival is typically experienced as a transpersonal force or fate--surpassing human agency--that carries its bearer along with it. It is characteristic that the person who is thus swept up will tend to intellectualize rather than to feel, and take responsibility for the chain of events which led to the unexpected, explosive recognition. Part of the reason will be that the disjunction between the pace of life which had been lived in relative obscurity and the new accelerated tempo engendered by the manic onrush of public accolade will be too vast to be experienced as real. Even when the discontinuity is perfectly concrete--as it is for example between the building of a bomb which may take years and the detonation of it, which may take a fraction of a second--it is difficult to psychologically connect two events of profoundly discordant tempos, as being but different phases of a unitary process. Thus, the explosion of a bomb, although one knows better, can seem to be but the arbitrary abstract outcome of all the years that went into the manufacture of it. It is an entirely different matter when we are trying to link up the explosive end product of a phenomenon such as fame with a largely unknown and incorporeal process that preceded it. As a result of this incomprehensible discontinuity, someone who, as Bobby, suddenly finds himself becoming famous will have to accustom himself to a radically accelerated pace of living and of relating, both intrapsychically and interpersonally. (A common self-perception is that things which used to take seemingly forever are now accomplished in a flash: e.g., Bobby--who used to work an entire year in order to earn five thousand dollars income as a freelance musician--at the peak of his popularity could command a fee of twenty thousand dollars for just an hour's work.)

5. A feeling of being more invincible than one has ever thought possible. As Freud observed long ago, when the ego perceives itself to be sufficiently hated, it can begin to believe it is in the process of dying (thus precipitating melancholia). Conversely, when the ego perceives itself as superabundantly loved, it can begin to believe it is beyond mortal harm (thus precipitating mania). Not surprisingly, Freud considered both melancholia and mania to be two pathological sides of the same coin. By contrast, when there is an onset of legitimate fame, it is a fact that a single person may become superabundantly loved by many and that this may become psychically tantamount to a sense of being more than mortal. This is beyond cockiness, it is instead the offshoot of a kind of psychic buffer which has arisen from the state of being bathed in multitudinous adulation surpassing one's wildest imagination. Seen this way, someone who has become truly famous could be described as someone who is thereby experiencing an *objective mania*.

6. A perception of the aura of fame beginning to surround oneself as being akin to a psychic entity, an outer source of potential adulation, attention, stimulation or threat so real that it can be felt as a palpable but invisible presence. Because of this, the onset of fame is often experienced as an almost altered state of consciousness that may include a sense of doubling of selves. (Since there is generally a profound incompatibility between the persona that is rapidly crystallizing in the eyes of the public and the anonymous face in the crowd one always took oneself to be, there is a necessity at some point for rethinking and perhaps realigning: which of the two is the true self and which is the false self?)

7. And, finally, there is the paranoia that can be the outcome of any of a number of radical changes one is undergoing: the unparalleled sense of public exposure; the inevitable dread, after awhile, of never being alone; the claustrophobic fear of being suffocated by unrelenting attention. As has already been suggested, a basic sense of interpersonal security is derived from the fact that an individual can bank on being able, in most social situations, to achieve a kind of reciprocity of psychical information flow: i.e., I tell you as much as I think you tell me, or as much as I feel is safe to tell you. This ability to regulate the exchange of personal

information--so commonplace as to be taken for granted--is completely ruptured in the case of the person who has become so well known that his reputation is sure to precede him. From this standpoint, every stranger he encounters has him at a distinct disadvantage: having already been privy to numerous vivid alleged personifications, whether accurate or inaccurate, to which he or she has undoubtedly internally responded. To the extent that the subject towards whom these responses have been directed, will not have had a chance to exert corrective feedback, he will be at their mercy. From the paranoid perspective of the famous person, an encounter with a stranger can therefore seem like a blind date with someone you know nothing about, but who may have been studying or stalking you for years. As ordinary people, we are so accustomed to focusing on our familiar wariness, vis-a-vis people whom we do not know, that we overlook the power--derived from being ourselves also part of the unknown--that we have over every stranger we meet. This becomes, however, glaringly apparent in the rare circumstance of the person who, like Bobby, discovers he is rapidly being shorn of the power which comes from being publicly unknown and therefore safely strange to nearly everyone you encounter.

TALK RADIO

Perhaps a personal story, concerning my one and only tiny brush with fame, can further illustrate the peculiar nature of the relationship we are discussing. It came shortly after the publication of my recent book, *The Portrait of the Artist as a Young Patient*, when a local radio station invited me to appear as a featured guest on a talk show program. I was to speak on the subject on which I was presumed to be an expert--the undiscovered young artist who has come to New York City in order to realize his or her dream of purchasing stardom--and I would be allocated a full half an hour of precious air time in which to articulate my point of view. Meanwhile, I had been informed by my publisher's publicist that talk radio is favored by book-lovers, even over televised author-interviews, and therefore was an ideal vehicle for introducing my book to the broadest possible audience.

So, on the one hand, viewed from a purely practical standpoint, I had everything to gain and nothing to lose by agreeing to go on the radio for the very first time. On the other hand, since practicality of any sort had never been a motive in writing the book--I wanted instead to express my personal vision of the vicissitudes of the creative outsider in America, as personified by the struggling young artist--the prospect of doing it simply in order to boost sales, was not especially enticing. Much more important was the possibility of expressing myself, of speaking about my book in a way that I had never done before, and to an audience that I would otherwise never reach.

And it was my dread of failing in a venture that therefore held so much meaning for me, and to which I did not have a clue as to whether I would be good or bad, eloquent as I hoped, or tongue-tied as I feared, that made my decision by no means automatic. But, of course, I agreed to go on the show, telling myself that I had to and that it would be cowardice not to, reminding myself that, after all, speaking one-on-one was my forte and that addressing an invisible audience in the confines of a lonely broadcast booth should pose no serious threat.

I tend to be a thoughtful person, who likes to prepare, so the night before my debut I tried to imagine what could not be imagined--the back and forth conversational flow between my interlocutor and myself--and I even privately embarrassed myself by writing down on a sheet of paper a series of pithy one-liners, concerning key points of my book, which I planned to "spontaneously" insert if and when the occasion arose.

Although I was initially taken aback by the state-of-the-art recording studio to which I was cordially conducted the next morning, I was also immediately reassured by the presence of my talk show host. Small and dynamic, she had paid her dues as a former reporter who had conscientiously combed the streets of New York searching for newsworthy stories. Now, as the star of a Sunday morning radio program that was beamed to an estimated seventy five thousand listeners in the Tri-State area, she exuded warmth, benign curiosity and almost unlimited confidence in her ability to maintain a conversation on the airwaves ("I can talk about anything for an hour.")

Maybe because I wanted to, I found myself believing her and I was further reassured when she showed the good sense to tell me in advance the questions she intended to pose when the initial taping began. I decided to put myself into her capable hands and trust that she at any rate knew what she was doing.

Yet, no matter how much she prepared me, no matter how much I tried to remind myself that this was not live radio and that, besides, I knew my book better than anyone else--there was no way I could have anticipated the mini-shock, or quantum jump as I have called it, that must be dealt with as one moves from the cocoon of anonymity to the scary open-ended space of broad public exposure.

In the case of radio, such a transition occurs in less than a second and you either sink (become victim to "mike fright") or swim. While I fortunately did not sink, and managed to do my share of conversational swimming, I had almost no idea at the conclusion of the thirty-minute taping session, as to how my performance would be received by the mysterious, but real audience to whom it would be broadcast in two weeks' time. I was therefore both relieved and grateful when my host nodded enthusiastic approval at the end of the interview, said, "Excellent, I won't change or edit a word," and proceeded to hand me as my personal reward a cassette of what had just been transacted.

In retrospect, my tiny brush with fame had presented me with three great surprises. The first was the radical transformation of consciousness that takes place when one is suddenly immersed into the realm of broad and lightning-fast public exposure: it was like nothing I had ever experienced. The second was that in some peculiar but undeniable way, it had been *thrilling*. (This was a special revelation to me inasmuch as I consider myself, like many therapists, to be a private person who treasures his privacy: someone who, whatever other shortcomings he may have, is not an exhibitionist.)

The third surprise--beyond doubt, the most disconcerting--was that there was little congruence between my subjective perception of what I was trying to say and how I thought I was actually coming across, and the so-called objective record as memorialized in the cassette. At least that is what I thought as I submitted to the humbling experience of listening to my radio persona for the very first time, which is not unlike having an out-of-body experience wherein you are uncannily allowed to perceive yourself as others do. And what I perceived, I initially barely recognized, or rather, did not want to recognize: a voice so filled with hesitations, repetitious phrases and unfinished trains of thought, that I could not imagine anyone being captured by it, let alone bowled over, as I had fantasized. Ruefully, as I marvelled at the melodious assurance of nearly every syllable enunciated by my interlocutor, I remembered her candid confession that she had not found the time to read my book. Had therefore all the years of earnest feeling and thought that I believed to have been compressed into this book, been--at least on this memorable public occasion--to no avail? Had I really been this ineffectual, or was I merely overreacting to the novel threat of imminent public exposure? For my answer, I appealed to my wife who had listened by my side, with whom I had been intimately and almost daily discussing the contents of my book for a period of years, and who, I was convinced, knew me better than anyone else. Her reply, immediately forthcoming, was as uncomplicated as my questioning of her had been torturous: "Yes, you were nervous in the beginning, understandably. But that was *you*. That's how you talk."

Those few words, given that I knew how much she genuinely loved to listen to whatever I had to say, were indescribably confirming. They enabled me to let go of my fleeting and entirely uncharacteristic aspiration to be a radio personality, and to summon the courage to listen a second time to what I had prematurely surmised had been a desolate performance. And, to my final surprise--after conceding that I was, after all, untrained and unpolished in the art of elocution--I realized in this second listening that what had come through had been what really mattered the most to me: I had said what I really wanted to say, I had been heartfelt about what I had said, and I had expressed myself in the way that suited me the best.

THE IDENTITY OF FAME

The realization I took away from my tiny brush with fame was that, although profound changes are indeed involved, *they do not have anything to do with intimacy.* If anything, as was confirmed in the case of those extraordinary individuals who, like Bobby, achieved authentic stardom, these changes moved them in the opposite direction. This can be understood if it is realized that the impact or shock of being a high profile figure can be repeated in the lifetime of a truly famous person many thousands of times.

When that occurs, the state of being famous becomes an *identity*, and it is an identity that differs significantly from others. The first difference is that-- since it cannot possibly keep up with or keep track of the pace of public validation--it is an after-the-fact identity. This is in contrast to all so-called normal ego identity formation which is more or less a product of and congruent with the degree of familial, social and peer group affirmation it receives.

Furthermore, because the media has been interposed between the famous person and his perception of his impression on others, *the crucial feedback of validation or invalidation has been effectively removed from the ego's control and transferred to an external source.*

So that, whereas in ordinary identity formation there is a more or less uninterrupted feedback loop running between self and other, in the case of the person who is famous there is necessarily a considerable delay in the reaction time of the public, and a response that, when it comes, is always, to some degree, externally censored. The image, therefore, that the self may truly want to project on the other--since in substantial measure it will have been appropriated by a media industry consumed with its own marketing and economic needs--may never even get projected in the first place. One fallout of this is that the self-perception of the person who is famous will be much more subject to the vicissitudes of large group dynamics than to the effects or lessons of familial or interpersonal interactions, which is the usual process.

In the normal course of development of one's identity, perhaps the closest analogy to what we are describing are those times when a peer group (typically in school years or in adolescence) will produce a supposedly consensually validated picture of a given individual's persona. But here again, the crucial difference is that there is access to immediate feedback from the group's evolving perception and, therefore, to at least the possibility of on-the-spot corrective measures. No such second chance for image control exists in the case of the famous person who, being generally absent at the time of its inception, will be helpless to ameliorate or transmute those elements of a public persona which are perceived as ego-alien but which have begun to harden.

For this reason--the lack of immediate reinforcing feedback from a public perception that is rapidly coalescing--the identity of fame can seem to its bearer a magical, transpersonal or archetypal existential state that has arrived for totally arbitrary reasons. On the other hand, since being famous typically represents the greatest possible public acclamation imaginable, it can assume, over time, the aura of a canonization. Compared with the normally slow increments of social approbation or disapproval which go into the consolidation of one's personal ego identity, the acquisition of legitimate fame can seem like an official reward conferred by society for some huge accomplishment (which, of course, is balanced by the paranoid doubt, "Can this really be happening to me?")

There is a sense, then--to be sure, always ambivalent--in which the identity of fame is equated with some measurable and quantifiable achievement (which in turn is then, literally, numerically calibrated: number of sales, popularity poll ratings, bankability) and to that degree can feel quite unreal. When that happens, the self-esteem and ego identity which existed prior to the attainment of fame, and which until then was primarily felt to be an attribute of the inner world, is experienced as being *brazenly appropriated and captured by an unknown public.*

Because fame, no matter how serendipitously it comes, is almost always the product of many hands (marketing, public relations, sales) sooner or later it will feel tainted and phony. To the degree that its lineage can be directly traced to the aggressive selling and manipulation of one's true self, it will seem as if it is--and must be--only a false self which is being applauded. And from that standpoint, the often plainly neurotic desire to hang on for dear life to the newly acquired identity as a famous person can begin to feel as though one is laboring to perpetuate a false self, that was thrust upon oneself, and from which one can no longer escape.

Today, because the escalating costs of high tech production are forcing artistic products, like any other products, to be bottom-line marketable, there is an unavoidable tendency--in order to cover the huge overhead--to standardize (i.e., make popular) art. The more this is so, the more art is targeted for mass consumption, and the more commercial it becomes. The most commercial art, economically speaking, is that which earns the greatest profit at the lowest cost. That is another way of saying that commercial art is that which receives or clearly aspires to receive much more than it gives. Which is the definition of narcissistic-giving art that we began with: by skillfully and convincingly contriving to promise far more than it delivers, if often succeeds, in the short run, in getting more than it deserves.

It should be obvious, in the context of this book, that the relationship of fame (whether as famous person to fan or unknown public, or as performing artist to audience) is a narcissistic-giving one par excellence. It is therefore no surprise that the popular or commercial art which dominates our time will do all it can to exploit and to incorporate in its idiom such an available and powerful dynamism: that is, under the auspices of purveying famous plots (hinging on murder, betrayal, seduction, revenge, violence and sex) and famous stereotypes (masculine and feminine personifications that are deemed to be currently in demand) it will strive to persuade the mass audience that the oh-so-popular dramatic fare being shown--if only by the sheer dint of being famous--is thereby possessed of undeniable and grandiose value.

CHAPTER FOUR

Narcissistic Giving In The Mental Health Profession

THE ANALYTIC WORLD

As part of my long apprenticeship, I spent about ten years in a number of therapy training institutes in the supposed capital of the mental health profession in America (New York City). Along the way I managed to conduct about a thousand diagnostic intakes, culled from a cross section of the broadest conceivable patient population. Perhaps even more important, from the standpoint of my education, were the literally hundreds of informal but nevertheless intense, in-depth conversations I had, across the years, with dozens of neophyte, aspiring therapists, who, like myself, could think of nothing better to do than to ventilate pent-up feelings about how it really felt to be a student therapist in a prestigious professional training institute.

While this is a vast subject in itself, worthy of a book, and here is not the place to go into detail, I would like to extract from a decade's experiences just a few principal points that pertain to the issue of narcissistic giving in the mental health profession.

In the past, this issue has been addressed in basically one of three ways: the journalistically debunking way of a Janet Malcolm; the sensationalistic exposé way--epitomized by Jeffrey Masson; and the self-serving, self-protective way of the mental health professional, where the vicissitudes of the self (i.e., the countertransference) are so cautiously rendered that they come to resemble sanitized puppet figures rather than human beings.

In other words, the issue of narcissistic giving in the mental health profession has not really been dealt with, or, to put it more accurately, it has been politicized. From the outside, by journalists who are invested in creating story lines that promise to gratify the prurient reading tastes of the general public who seem most interested in the most lurid details of psychoanalysis and psychotherapy. And from the inside, by an elite corps of writing professionals who are even more heavily invested in disseminating a made-to-order image of themselves and their skills, the primary purpose of which is to insure self-preservation.

Such political bickering, of course--attack from the outside, defense from the inside--serves only to muddy the issue at hand: which is, what is everyone fighting about in the first place? Although I am aware there is no simple, unitary answer to this question, I would like to encapsulate, especially after immersing myself for ten years in the ideological battlefields of the mental health profession, what I think I have learned:

Perhaps foremost is this: if it is true that psychotherapy is an art--a proposition to which the majority of therapists give lip service, but which I take seriously--then it follows that the chances of becoming a good psychotherapist simply by entering the tightly structured and doctrinaire world of the training institute are roughly comparable to the chances of becoming a good short story writer by enrolling in a creative writing program. It also follows that the very qualities that would enable one to rise to an institute position of political or administrative power are almost antithetical to the qualities that are needed to nurture the creative core of the developing psychotherapist. This is because the creative nurturing of students has almost nothing to do with the skills that are required in order to obtain and to hold on to political power in an institute. If this is so, and I have no doubt it is, it means that the stated purpose of training institutes--to inaugurate a process that will regularly turn out accomplished therapists--is doomed to abort soon after its inception. It further means that even the finest training institutes, despite their best intentions, will not only tolerate characterological deformities of the therapeutic personality which is the desideratum, but will unwittingly produce such therapeutic anomalies.

Because of this, sooner or later, every mental health professional--and I have found no exception to this rule in the hundreds of intimate conversations I have engaged in with aspiring therapists of every rank--arrives at the sad realization that the world of therapy as it is portrayed in the abstract and as it exists in the flesh, simply do not coincide. If it is borne in mind that the typical beginning therapist enters into the field, first, in order to understand himself or herself, and, second, in order to be truly understood, then it may be appreciated just how devastating it is to encounter esteemed professionals who seem far more interested in people in the abstract than in *you*. Seen this way, it is not surprising that, with few exceptions, the idealistic neophyte will at some point come to feel profoundly ungiven to.

Occasionally, of course, there is the great teacher, but in my experience you are lucky if you meet even one truly inspirational person during the time it takes (usually years) to be awarded a fellowship from a postgraduate training institute or a diploma from an academic clinical program. Very often a student can successfully complete such a program of advanced instruction in how to be a psychotherapist without feeling a single valuable therapeutic connection had ever been made. What does this mean when the primary learning experience by which one supposedly becomes an effective therapist--and which, as is commonly agreed, will shape and leave its mark on nearly everything that succeeds it--is one in which the neophyte feels profoundly ungiven to?

It means that a certain hopelessness concerning the capacity to professionally nurture another will eventually, consciously or unconsciously, creep into the mindset of the evolving therapist when it comes time to practice and to try his or her hand on others. After all, to a great extent the fundamental model for helping others will be taken from and will reflect the help which one received during the critical period of one's own professional apprenticeship. If that model, upon which one draws and depends in moments of stress and uncertainty, is perceived as basically unnourishing (as it typically is) then the fledgling therapist will be in a position that is painfully analogous to the first-time parent whose own childhood memories are replete with unmistakable evidence of abuse.

PATTERNS OF DEVALUATION

The abuse that the beginning therapist experiences, as he or she launches into the rigorous training program required for professional certification, is, of course, never physical, as is often the case in abusive relationships, and only rarely is it even overtly verbal. Instead, it is much more refined, devious and cerebral. In the ten years I spent in training institutes I can honestly say that no one ever raised his or her voice to me, used language that was insulting or profane, or departed in any flagrant manner from a code of conduct considered becoming for a professional. When speaking, therefore, of the kind of abuse that the novice therapist is likely to incur, it is more appropriate to talk about sins of omission--patterns of student neglect so persistent that over time it can only feel like a covert act of devaluation.

This goes back, of course, to the sad realization that the world of therapy as it is portrayed in the abstract and as it exists in the flesh, simply do not coincide. For it quickly becomes apparent that the primary concern and preoccupation of training institutes is with the fulfillment of its own needs and aims which--declarations of having been founded for the express purpose of facilitating the developmental growth of budding therapists notwithstanding--have very little to do with the needs of students.

Accordingly, as a rule, teaching professionals are far more interested in demonstrating to themselves, to their peers, and to spectating others that they are indeed teaching well--that is, in conformance to their own idiosyncratic, narcissistic standards--than (what it should be obvious is considerably more important in a training facility) that students are *learning well* (which at times may require that a teacher relinquish a preferred teaching technique that is not working for a more prosaic one that might work).

Perhaps nowhere is the indifference of prominent teaching professionals more in display than in the written evaluations they are obligated to submit at the end of the semester for each and every student: evaluations which, upon request, are read to the recipients. If it is borne in mind that from the standpoint of the expectant student much is at stake, and that such evaluations are therefore meant to convey in a pithy and profound manner the precise level of growth of an evolving therapist--then I think it is safe to say they may be also read as indicators of the teacher's commitment to the welfare of his or her students. Having said that, let me briefly parade some sample and very typical evaluations, culled from the student days of myself and my colleagues as we jointly submitted to the demanding regimen of the training institute:

"Participates enthusiastically in class discussion."

"Would benefit from some more clinical experience."

"Possesses an incisive mind, but I'm not sure if she has the determination necessary for the long haul . . ."

"Has a very therapeutic personality and is a pleasure to be with . . ."

When it is remembered that each of the above evaluations, and hundreds more like them, were composed by undoubtedly intelligent, sensitive and highly esteemed teaching professionals, then I think the conclusion is inescapable that the remarkable banality which is their primary characteristic must be attributed to either profound indifference, or impairment of the capacity to nurture prospective therapists.

THE SELLING OF MENTAL HEALTH

I believe the greatest contaminant of both the teaching and the practice of psychotherapy is the *economic* one: the fact that, essentially, it is conceived of as a service delivered for a fee. Crucial consequences flow from this. If psychotherapy at bottom is an art, as I contend, then what happens when it is professionalized is analogous to what happens when an artist is forced to earn his living solely from his art--*it becomes commercialized.* Now, while it is widely recognized that there are unwanted side effects which go hand in hand with the commercialization of art--it will seek out the lowest common denominator in popular taste, shamelessly aim to please and placate, divert itself from the primary task of facilitating and articulating its inner idiom in order to search for strategies designed to exploit promising buying trends--it is somehow overlooked that comparable damage is rendered when psychotherapy becomes commercialized. This is because, as I have mentioned, although lip service is given to the maxim that psychotherapy is an art, it is, instead, predominantly regarded and pursued as a middle class occupation, something chosen primarily in order to secure an economic base for one's life. As such, it is forged by the competitive dynamics of the mental health marketplace and it is subject to the restrictions, role definitions and expectations as imposed by the marketplace consumers of psychotherapy. For his part, the mental health professional who dutifully adheres to the standardized practices of his occupation, over time, can expect to earn a degree of prestige and, above all, to be rewarded with a regular income and lasting security.

As noted, none of this applies to the practice of authentic art and it is a measure of the extent to which the creative core of psychotherapy is regularly dismissed that the professionalization and commercialization of psychotherapy continues unimpeded and at breakneck pace. Another factor, which has greatly blurred the damage done to the art of psychotherapy by commercializing it, has been the ongoing medicalization of the mental health profession. This is easy to understand once it is recognized that the antithesis of relating to another person in a creative manner is to apply a technique of relating to the other as a specimen or object--the basis of the medical model. To the degree that psychotherapy (with psychoanalysis historically leading the way in this country) has allowed itself to be governed by the medical model, it has striven more and more to emulate the gaudy technical successes and innovations that are the hallmark of modern medicine. The result has been the elevation, and even canonization of technique in psychotherapy as being something external, perfectible and replicable in the manner of traditional medical practices. With that the irony has ensued that while on the one hand there has to be objectivity (and therefore some technique) in the practice of psychotherapy, on the other hand, nothing is perhaps more injurious to the possibility of two people authentically and intimately meeting than for one of them to come armed to the encounter with a technique for relating, a technique in which one often has been assiduously trained for many years.

Is this a brief for a restorative socialization of the mental health profession, as a means of returning it to its lost creative integrity? On the contrary, the therapists I have known who have been afforded the greatest economic and job security--generally from working for assorted governmental agencies--on the whole, have been among the least inspired and most uncommitted. I think the reason for this is fairly obvious: while it is alright to pursue a middle class lifestyle (as do most therapists, including myself) predicated upon economic security, it is not alright to introduce such economic middle class values when attempting to engage in a deep way the layers of the human psyche. Although inextricably mixed in this century, commercialism and the psyche, as encountered in the analytic situation, have always been strange bedfellows. Intense, passionate, ethical involvement--a genuine non-materialistic love for the creative intimate work of psychotherapy--is the only thing I know which can counteract the corrosive technological pull of the economic contaminant; and this, of course, by definition, occurs rarely.

TECHNIQUE AS NARCISSISTIC GIVING

When I look back upon the years I spent in training institutes, it seems to me that a considerable portion of the feelings of deprivation and unnecessary frustration I and many of my friends were experiencing as we struggled to meet the requirements, and answer the challenges steadily imposed upon us--could be attributed to narcissistic giving: specifically, the idea of the misuse of *technique as narcissistic giving*.

Such misuse of technique was fairly widespread among therapists I knew and therapeutic institutes I had contact with. It was bolstered by the belief that somehow merely by practicing a particular recommended technique, and presumably knowing how to do it, you were thereby benefitting a patient or a student; and I came to consider that the biggest fallacy and weakness of the institute teaching professionals. In their compulsion to teach what is teachable, they would often so fixate on the designated principle of technique, that they would in the process lose sight of the purpose of it all. There was another factor: because in our society there is a tendency to defer to the putative expert, it is relatively easy for mental health professionals to tap into the built-in readiness of students and patients to view them as authentically grandiose beings. This is another way of saying that sometimes it is seductively tempting for mental health professionals to feel they have discharged their responsibility by simply *acting grandiose* (without actually having given anything to their patients).

Let me give you, out of hundreds, just a few examples of what I mean by technique as narcissistic giving:

In a world-renowned mental health center in New York City, there is, or was for many years, a preferred seating arrangement for therapy sessions in which patient and therapist are obligated to sit side by side one another. The technical rationale behind this peculiar, nearly parallel seating position, was that by so doing you were making an efficient compromise between the distraction of eye-to-eye contact (as in psychoanalytic psychotherapy) and the presumed impersonality of immediately lying on the couch (as in classical psychoanalysis). Yet, after having briefly attended this same world-renowned institute as a patient and thereby experiencing it first hand, it had immediately struck me as patently stilted: two people, talking and trying to relate by peeking out of the corners of their eyes at one another--and I had concluded whatever benefit might come from avoiding direct eye-to-eye contact would quickly be erased by the artificiality of the so-called technical solution.

But that was only my opinion, the opinion of someone who at the time was a student therapist. I could test it, however, by seeing how it stacked up against other experiences of patients, culled from the one thousand diagnostic intakes I eventually conducted. And because this peculiar, nearly parallel seating arrangement between patient and therapist favored by this famous mental health center was such a precise detail, such an isolated variable, it afforded a priceless opportunity to try and measure it. Accordingly, whenever I encountered a former patient from this same mental health center who wanted to discuss his or her past therapy, I invariably would inquire about the seating arrangement. Without exception, they responded it made them feel uncomfortable, seemed alienating, added distance between them and their therapists, and in no way aided therapy.

Although this parallel seating arrangement is only a single detail, it is an excellent example of what I call technique as narcissistic giving. Someone, or some group of people with perhaps the best intentions in the world, a long time ago believed that parallel seating might actually facilitate a therapeutic relationship, that it was indeed an advance in technique. A policy was perhaps adopted, encouraged and enforced. Teachers were so advised, who passed it on to their students, who also passed it on and a generation of patients were obliged "for their own good" to peek sideways at their therapists who also were advised to peek sideways back at them.

That's just one example of how technique, if sufficiently divorced from the web-like complexity of shifting human interaction so as to be reified, can become itself, inadvertently iatrogenic, an instance of narcissistic giving.

Here's another:

In another famous therapy center in New York City--in an endeavor to cross-culture psychiatry--there is a policy of admitting psychiatrists or psychologists from diverse cultures into their prestigious training program; and, occasionally, patients, usually those who pass through their low-cost clinic, will be assigned one of those therapists from a distinctly different culture.

It sounds fine on paper, and humanistic, too, to gather together therapists from scattered, disconnected cultures and provide them the opportunity to really learn firsthand the American way of life by working directly with American patients. The only problem with this is that patients, although they are characteristically too submissive to complain, almost invariably hate to be treated by someone from a culture they do not understand.

Put yourself in their shoes. It is difficult enough meeting a complete stranger, attempting to be candid about your most intimate thoughts and feelings and somehow believing a complete stranger is going to understand, even accept you. If you add to that the fact the stranger is also a stranger from a strange land, someone who immediately strikes you as having no intuitive grasp of your basic way of life, it cannot help but pose an additional enormous strain upon the already considerable ordinary one of trusting your therapist. Not surprisingly in the one thousand diagnostic intakes I conducted--where I was routinely required to elicit individual preferences concerning their prospective therapist--*I never once encountered a patient who asked for a therapist from an unfamiliar culture.*

One last example:

There is an unwritten rule in the American Mental Health field that the less economic power a patient has, the worse treatment he or she is offered. Institutes, mental health centers, and hospitals typically assign to their poorest patients their least experienced therapists, and to their richest patients, their most prestigious therapists. Although lip service is officially given to the credo that therapists are assigned according to the patient's needs, that is usually not how it works. Abuses to powerless patients are most clearly seen, as was pointed out long ago by Thomas Szasz, in the framework of psychiatric institutions which not only wield the greatest power but traditionally cater to the most powerless (because most helplessly disturbed) of patients.

I had an opportunity to observe this years ago, when I worked in the first state-funded alcoholism rehabilitation unit situated on the premises of Creedmoor Psychiatric Center. As a team member, I was obliged to partake in so-called group screening interviews of recently detoxified alcoholics. A group interview is just what it sounds like--instead of one pair of strange eyes examining you, there are a group of strange eyes. As for the group interview, it often comes down to a series of unintentionally humiliating questions--meant to ascertain the degree of organicity or brain damage that can often result from chronic alcoholism--such as: "Starting from one hundred, subtract seven, and keep subtracting seven until you can't anymore" or "Starting with our current president, and working backwards, name the last five presidents."

I participated in several dozen of such group screening interviews, and I never saw one I thought did the least bit of therapeutic good for the patient. But

116

that is the point. No one seemed to be thinking clearly and directly about the patient's benefit. The idea was that the group interview, by achieving an almost instantaneous cross-fertilization of interdisciplinary team members, was, of course, benefiting the patient inasmuch as it was bestowing upon him or her the benefit of the group interview technique. It is an almost perfect example of technique as narcissistic giving: by "giving" the patient the benefit of the supposedly efficacious group interview technique, psychiatric institutions were able to overlook the disturbing fact that such group interviews, as experienced by the patient, were almost always deflating and humiliating. In an analogous fashion, it may be that well-meaning prestigious therapy centers believe that they are giving the poor patient the benefit of the technique of the cross-cultural psychiatrist, or of the parallel seating arrangement, while disregarding the depressing and untherapeutic impact, as I believe, such stilted practices invariably have.

THERAPEUTIC PERSONALITY AND THE GIFT OF THE THERAPEUTIC ENCOUNTER

By now it should be obvious that I believe that disembodied technique--that is not seamlessly woven into the web of the therapist's creative true self--is not only ineffectual, but at times harmful. Yet, curiously, in today's climate where the mental health profession tends more and more to compartmentalize therapy, the therapist and technique--and thereupon to externalize and laud technique for its alleged machine-like proficiency--that is what repeatedly happens: psychotherapists who are seriously cut off from their feelings but are reputed to be admirable technicians, are not only allowed to survive, they are often rewarded and promoted.

But if it is not disembodied, externalized and machine-like technique that is to facilitate a genuinely therapeutic encounter for the patient, if it is something that spontaneously emerges from the creative true self of the therapist--then what are its attributes?

While every therapist will have his or her own list, here (as I wrote in *Portrait of the Artist as a Young Patient*) is mine:

"1. *Therapeutic personality (which includes warmth)*. First of all, it is obvious that someone can be their creative, spontaneous, alive true self and still be nasty (if that is part of their true self). So the true self must be therapeutic. And now we can immediately define what we mean by a therapeutic personality. *A therapeutic personality is a true self whose presence is therapeutic.*

2. *Empathic imagination.* You can be a good doctor without imagination. You can be a good physicist without imagination. But you can't be a good therapist without imagination. It takes imagination to leap nimbly from self to self and then back again. Kohut's (1978) important concept of introspective empathy and the empathic stance seems to take for granted the critical factor of imagination. Empathic is always empathic imagination. To be always anxiously attending to the needs of a narcissistic or depressed mother does not in itself make for empathy, it can also make for being excessively attentive to the needs of the other. To turn it into true empathy, to be able to objectively see and understand the other's world through the other's eyes, requires the kind of imaginative leap made, for example, by the writer who, with only limited experience and observation of another's existence, can sometimes vividly reconstruct a chunk of a life. That is why true empathy is more than a trait or a personality profile. It is a gift of imagination.

3. *Kindness.* It is so taken for granted that the quality of kindness is an important ingredient in therapeutic, human relating that it is never spoken about. We have to go outside analytic literature to find a prominent author who takes kindness seriously as a topic worth writing about--all the way to Kurt Vonnegut (1982). Yet it is a sad fact that there are people who habitually frequent training institutes who are not kind. They may not be iatrogenic or abrasive, but neither do they possess any manifest degree of kindness that seems appropriate to the special poignancy that each patient in his or her unique way brings to the treatment, and sometimes is the *only* sensitive intervention. Patients, of course, will stick it out for years with an unkind therapist--if only because it recreates a familiar scenario between themselves and an indifferent parent--but one wonders, without the benefit of a benign, therapeutic introject, how much progress can really be made.

118

4. *Clinical sensibility and artistry.* This is not to deny a place for competent, though uninspired therapy. A therapist with a basic sense of self, some sensitivity, and a certain good fellowship--but no special breadth of clinical sensibility or gift of artistry--can definitely carry a patient (someone who is suffering and ready to make a connection) farther than he or she was before entering treatment. But not much farther. Because of this (and many other traits) good training institutes are aware that what the candidate brings to the institute is more important than what the institute brings to the candidate. But institutes do not talk about what cannot be taught (naturally). They only talk about what can be taught. It is natural that a false equation gets set up in the minds of trainees: technique equals that which is taught; and that which is not taught is not technique. On the contrary, *the technique that cannot be taught is more important than the technique that can be taught.* This does not mean to challenge the place of good training and a good institute, which is invaluable. A candidate can no more make himself or herself into a true analyst than a patient can execute a legitimate self-cure. It does mean that Lang's frame, no matter how expertly administered, unless it, *in turn, is framed or held in the therapeutic (whatever those qualities may be) true self of a good analyst will have little or no impact on a patient."*

Increasingly today, press coverage is devoted to therapists who, allegedly, shamelessly break the rules of professional conduct. Yet far more common, because much more insidious, are therapists who lifelessly, mechanistically, dehumanistically, and obsessive-compulsively *enforce* the rules.

CHAPTER FIVE

Intimate Giving

REVERSAL

We have now arrived at the focal point of this brief study, and the reason I wrote the book. If narcissistic giving is a contemporary paradigm, as I believe, of the antipode of intimate giving, then by an imaginative but simple process of reversal, a revealing if rough sketch of the character of true nurturance and mature intimacy should emerge. With this in mind, I propose to reexamine a number of earlier examples and to make explicit its healthy antithesis. Finally, I would like to suggest that by so doing some general properties may be extracted that can help clarify what it means to be intimately giving.

1. In the opening example there is a description of the plight of my friend, who, becoming panicked when the book upon which he had worked for years had initially failed to sell, went to his publisher's publicist. What he most feared was that somehow his publisher had lost confidence in him, deciding they had made a mistake to believe in him in the first place, and had covertly decided to cut their losses by not bothering to promote him. In order to reassure himself this was not the case, he respectfully but pointedly inquired of the publicist as to the nature and extent of the efforts that were being made on behalf of his book. For his trouble, he was made to feel as though he were being somewhat obsessive as the publicist--who treated him in a lighthearted manner throughout--ended their conversation by reminding him that she had "been doing publicity for years".

As I showed, this was magnificently beside the point. What the author needed, perhaps first of all, was sensitive recognition that he was undergoing a genuine crisis of confidence regarding the fate of his beloved book, as it seemed to be reflected in the startlingly dismal sales figures. There were a variety of ways this could have been done, but a simple and sincere "I can see that you're very disappointed" might have sufficed. Second, whatever realistically positive

120

information that might have suggested a brighter future for the book, should have been presented in detail. And third, some kind of heartfelt commitment to the book on the part of the publicist (which, of course, was supposedly part of her job duties) was sorely needed and, therefore, might have gone a long way. (Reversal in this example thereby gives us at least one important property which pertains to all intimate giving: it does not, in any way, minimize, shrink or reduce the needs of the other).

2. The second example of the book is drawn from my private practice as a psychotherapist in New York City. It was related to me by Sarah--a psychotherapist, herself, who happened to be in supervision with me at the time-- and it concerned one of her own patients whom she had encouraged, because of episodic suicidal fantasies, to seek out a psychiatric consultation in order to explore the possible need for anti-depressants.

As it turned out, Sarah's patient was a woman who was unduly wary of strangers, especially psychiatrists. Accordingly, she had made it crystal-clear on the telephone, prior to the consultation visit, that she already had a psychotherapist (Sarah) whom she liked very much and was therefore only looking for, at most, someone who might monitor her medication if this was required. Yet, such preparations notwithstanding, the ensuing session was an unmitigated disaster: the psychiatrist repeatedly challenging the veracity of the experiences she reported; calling into question the usefulness of the treatment she had received from her therapist; and, finally, as a coup de grace, upon learning that Sarah was *only* a psychoanalytic psychotherapist, triumphantly exclaiming, "So, you see, she's *not* a doctor!"

Here, one might way, the person is engaging in a more pernicious form of narcissistic giving. It is not only irrelevant to make a point of noting that her present therapist is not a doctor, it is subversive: the intent being, as subsequently became clear, to pave the way for the doctor to appropriate the patient. What the patient needed here, instead, was almost the exact opposite of what the consulting psychiatrist offered: someone who intuitively understood that it was important to respect her current therapeutic affiliation--as should have been evident from her initial guarded exploratory telephone call--and certainly not to compete with it. On a deeper level, given the patient was phobic regarding strangers, she needed to know that the psychiatrist was deserving of her trust, if she were able to muster it. Secondly, she needed to know if in addition to her usual routine of talk therapy there was a benefit to be gained from taking an antidepressant. And third, in view of her manifest suspicion of psychiatrists and their drugs, she needed to be given a sensitive and careful description of the benefits vs. costs (side effects) of any prospective drug she might be advised to try.

All of which, of course, was in marked contrast to the oneupmanship she was subjected to at the hands of a doctor who seemed bent on controlling her through the devious art of psychiatric devaluation. (This points to a second property of all intimate giving: that it primarily invests its energies in the needs of the other as opposed to its own. While this seems obvious, what is truly amazing is how often what passes for giving turns out, upon closer inspection, to be but a narcissistic giving detour towards blatant self-gratification.)

3. In the example of "The Wrong Gift" (p. 28) I return to the plight of my friend who, still frustrated by the continuing low sales of his book, had decided to take matters into his own hands. He had dedicated himself to a personal word-of-mouth campaign to publicize his book by assiduously contacting anyone he knew whom he thought might conceivably have a bearing on its distribution. What's more, he had begun to regularly contact his publisher's marketing manager at the beginning of each month to hear firsthand (from the latest computer printout) the number of his books which had been sold for the preceding thirty days. Accordingly, six months after it had been published, by which time a much clearer picture of his impact upon the general reading public should have been available, he once more inquired as to what the current sales figures revealed. To which the marketing manager, in an animated celebratory tone, proclaimed, "We sold 108 books for October, thanks mostly to your efforts."

Such a reply--given that both author and marketing manager were well aware that only 108 books sold nationwide for an entire month is, by any standard, shocking--is an instance of what might be called *tangential nurturing*: wherein the intent plainly is to provide a substitute gratification which can compensate the person enough to deflect his attention away from the inherent frustration in not being heard.

In the case of my friend, then, intimate giving, far from being a meaningless pat on the back purporting to congratulate him for his personal efforts on behalf of promoting his own book, would have first empathically addressed the undeniably discouraging picture presented by six months of consistently subpar sales figures. It would have conscientiously indicated what the author might expect of the second half of the year and it would have offered whatever realistic hopes there were for believing things might take a turn for the better. Recognizing that the author's faith in the public's acceptance of his book was understandably rapidly waning, it would have made a point of emphasizing both its loyalty to the venture and its undaunted determination to make it succeed. (Here is a third indispensable mark of intimate giving: it intuitively zeroes in on the primary need of the other; listens closely and intelligently with an eye towards what can constructively be done; and then, in good faith, does what it can.)

4. In the example of *Fail-Sale Relating* (p. 35), I draw upon my own experience as a fledgling author, when I was led down the garden path by a wily and ambitious editor who, although promising a great deal, as it turned out, had no intention of incurring the slightest personal risk. What I painfully learned from this episode (perhaps as intellectual solace) I subsequently dubbed "fail-safe relating": the endeavor, by making sure that one takes as little risk as possible-- to derive only benefits from interpersonal interactions. While it is easy to see, when put in these terms, that this is impossible, what is remarkable is how frequently people will attempt with the straightest of faces to pull this off. Part of the attraction must be that since nothing is going to be invested, nothing can be lost. Thus, in the worst case scenario in which none of the hoped-for benefits are forthcoming, there is always the consolation that one has only gambled on a no-lose interpersonal bet.

Intimate giving, in this instance, as I go on to remark, "as opposed to the pretense of watching out for both the interests of myself and my agent--would have been to have personally assumed the responsibility and risk for either publishing or not publishing my book and to have at some point directly communicated her honest intentions one way or the other." (It is yet another property of intimate giving that it accepts responsibility for the inescapable interpersonal risk that is entailed when someone elects to move close enough to another person so as to be in a position to sensitively help.)

CHARACTERISTICS

The reader can go through the other everyday examples and try the simple experiment of imagining what it would be like to be on the receiving end of the opposite of what is presented. Such an experiment, if faithfully carried out and, subsequently, thoughtfully reflected upon, will, I believe, reveal the following common characteristics of what, for want of a better name, I have been calling intimate giving:

As the preceding few examples show, an act of intimate giving begins with a clear focusing on the other's needs, implicit in which is an empathic reading of the underlying dynamics, which are often exceedingly complex, of the specific request. In order to have reached this position, however--the interpersonal vantage point from which someone can meaningfully and realistically be nurturing in even a seemingly trivial way to another person--it is necessary that one will have managed, at least temporarily, to have set aside normal but interfering selfish needs so as to be able to invest the required energy. Since the investment of energy can often be considerable, the individual must be prepared to spend a sufficient amount of *time*, and it is therefore a general characteristic of an act of intimate giving that before it is initiated, there will be a decision that, somehow, the appropriate time will be found. That is why the antipodal characteristic of impatience--which will be defined as an irritable attempt to hurry up a process which one feels, for a variety of reasons, promises only to frustrate instead of gratify one's desires--is a hallmark of narcissistic giving and a sure sign of the fundamentally bogus nature of its claim to be humanly available for someone else's anticipated needs.

It is important to realize that this conception of time is not measured, as time traditionally is, in standardized segments, but in terms of being available for as long as it takes to respond in a nurturing way: i.e., the clock it goes by is *developmental*. Thus, in the example of Molly, the painter (p. 45), who had been frustrated for months by the curator of an art gallery who had not bothered to look at her portfolio of slides--real giving could have been accomplished in only the time it took to say (sincerely) "Well, I regret I have been so backed up that I have been unable to get to it sooner as I promised. But it is sitting right here on top of the stack on my desk, and I really do promise you that I *will* get to it in about a week."

Because an act of intimate giving begins typically with a clear and in-depth perception of what is behind what the other seems to be asking for, it is almost always empathic in nature. It is never purely informational even when the other seems to be seeking nothing more consequential than, let us say, the correct time of day and the reason for this is that it is primarily concerned with the interpersonal context out of which the question emerges. So, for example, if the person requesting time is really expressing a sense of being somewhat

124

discouraged with the way *his or her time* is progressing, the other might--after purveying the desired information--also communicate, non-verbally, that there is an awareness that more is needed than just information. To put it another way, it is a mark of intimate giving that it sizes up, and takes into account, consciously or unconsciously, the relational and developmental possibilities that are present. In so doing, it transcends the immediate here and now need and anticipates the future.

In addition, intimate giving is:

1. *Congruent*: There is a matching of what is truly needed with what is really being given.

2. *Nurturing*. Although it is characteristically taken for granted in any posture of giving--that what is being offered is, of course, going to be helpful or at the very least is intended to be helpful--it is surprisingly rare when help that is given is even minimally nurturing. Real nurturing implies help that is more than patchwork--that is developmental inasmuch as it is capable of facilitating, via a timely and benign relationship, a person's progress in a healthy direction. Intimate giving, because of this, is more often tilted towards the developmental future (best long range interests of the individual) as opposed to the immediate assuagement of transient difficulties. It is therefore nurturing, and is perceived that way, in a sense that narcissistic giving or even legitimate but superficial helpfulness can never be. I think this is borne out by the fact--when you think about it--of how infrequent it is that someone has the experience of being really grateful for the right help being given at the right time.

3. *Meaningful*. Because an act of intimate giving generally strives to reach some part of the core of the other's psyche, it cannot be the meaningless experience that narcissistic giving essentially is.

4. *Reciprocal*. It is characteristic of an act of intimacy that it aspires to make contact with, resonate with, and to be known by as well as to know the other. From an interactive standpoint, therefore, it typically tends towards reciprocity. It is a tendency reinforced by an absence of a power-orientation, which traditionally has depended on the advantages conferred

by hierarchical distancing. The result is an intimate transaction whose center of gravity, more likely than not, will be the same for both parties.

5. *Revelatory.* When someone is deeply attuned to what the other wants-- in spite of the fact attention and energy seems directed away from the self--there is an inevitable and significant disclosure of who one is. By its nature intimacy entails a relaxation and readjustment of one's boundaries, that is prelude to the expansion of and flowing out of the self that is part of its process. To the degree that an act of intimacy entails such an expressive movement of the true self, it will tend to reveal what otherwise would be hidden or at least clouded by normal defensive operations.

6. *Serious.* As already shown, narcissistic giving employs a host of strategies designed to trivialize, diminish, shrink and reduce and other as a means of relieving the internalized pressure people feel to constantly interpersonally relate. By contrast, an intimate interaction is characterized by its intuitive grasp of what is most existentially pressing to the other. Accordingly, it cannot help but take the situation of the other seriously, respect it, and therefore use language, expeditiously as possible, to express issues of the self, and not--as is common in narcissistic giving--to erect a diverting non-communicative facade of desensitizing superficiality.

7. *Forthcoming.* Unlike narcissistic giving, which relies heavily upon tactics of emotional withholding, an intimate act is one in which a person elects to reduce the psychical distance between self and other in order to be in close enough range to make greater contact if desired, as well as to be taken in more fully by another who is so inclined. The result is that the receiver of intimate giving often has the novel experience of another self which is approaching or forthcoming but neither in an intrusive nor aggressive fashion.

8. *Binding.* Even a fleeting intimacy can have the effect of inaugurating a bond between two people--who previously otherwise were not connected--which can later be built upon. In this sense, intimacy is really a foundational glue that binds people together and is probably the best predictor of longevity in human relations. As an authentic bridge between

psyches it is resistant to normal interpersonal wear and tear and unlike its polar opposite--narcissistic giving--it does not tend, upon the first frontal attack, to crumble like a house of cards.

9. *Trusting*: At the core of the defense of narcissistic giving lurks the paranoid fear of being exposed--which in its extreme form leads to the interpersonal philosophy that offense is the best defense, with its concommitant strategy of the preemptive attack (p. 68). By contrast, trust is at the center, or at the very least at the beginning, of any interaction that can be designated as intimate. If one thinks about it, to enter into a relationship with another that is in any way congruent, nurturing, meaningful, reciprocal, revelatory (or possesses any of the traits thus far mentioned)--is also to take a risk. In most cases, the risk is not to one's flesh and bone but to a part of the self that has become unavoidably denuded through the act of being intimate. Inasmuch as there is danger, courage is required, and it is no small part of the reason people generally feel good about themselves after they have attempted to be intimate, that they know, on some level, that they have been uncharacteristically courageous. The trust that is involved, therefore, is that one--by having the courage to take the risk that is involved in being intimate--will not thereby hurt oneself in some unforeseen way. But trust, being a human attribute, is not only variable, but dynamically sensitive to the interpersonal context out of which it arises: which means, there is always a chance that it can seriously backfire. When it does, or when one thinks it does, there is the familiar dread that perhaps one has taken too big a risk, exposed oneself unnecessarily and in fact wrongly trusted. In its extreme form, such fears are indistinguishable from paranoia--the traumatic perception that far from strengthening oneself through a heightened and nurturing mutuality, one has actually laid oneself bare to an untrustworthy other. So, although trust, as I believe, is an indispensable constituent of an intimate act, there is a sense in which it is never far removed from and is linked to (if only as a negative potentiality) its inverse, paranoia.

10. *Profoundly personal*. Implicit in many narcissistic-giving transactions is the grandiose belief that efficient and productive impersonality can be

a suitable and sometimes complete substitute for the fundamental need of the self to be confirmed in any interpersonal encounter, no matter how fleeting; and that by offering the benefits to be plausibly derived from an impersonal, professional or business relationship you have thereby delivered something of such value that the need to relate in a genuinely human way can be justifiably relinquished. In sharp contrast to this, an instance of intimate giving, whatever else it may be, is always, on some level, profoundly personal. While it may also be realistic or objective, it is never abstract, dry or simply logical. It is not politicized. Regardless of the belief system that is held, there is the sense that the person is relating according to some distinctive inner logic that in turn is in harmony with his or her true self.

These are just some of the key traits that characterize intimate giving. There are others that have already been indirectly touched upon in the book. Intimate giving, for example, does not rely upon the tactics of power; does not attempt to gain deference through intimidation. It pursues, instead, from the other the respect that is freely given in response to an experience of being nurtured. It does not reduce complicated emotional requests, which may involve multi-determined, dynamic and often unconscious forces, to the status of pedestrian one-dimensional questions.

It does not employ sleight of hand. It is not subversive, bullying, or pseudo-logical. It is not an agent of the false self. It does not attempt to appear giving by courageously revealing a shameful trauma from the past. By contrast, the intimate disclosure that is a fundamental component of ongoing intimacy far transcends the simple, howsoever dramatic telling of painful, horrible secrets.

An act of intimate giving, as opposed to narcissistic giving, is a process rather than a one-time, cathartic experience. It is not a confession. It is not looking for release from pent-up childhood traumas. It is not the expression, or cultivation, of a "victim" identity. It is not melodramatically larger than life, sensationalistic or titillating.

When conflict is involved, it typically will hinge on the capacity, on the one hand, for reciprocal nurturing and, on the other, on the attendant anxieties concerning incorporation, transgression or dissolution of one's boundaries, and the paranoid fear of the dangers ensuing from too much closeness. What's more, such conflicts as do exist will be contained rather than acted out.

128

Finally, sensation will not be overvalued and pursued for its own sake. Relationships will not be viewed primarily as a means for the achievement of exciting experiences. Instead, they will be appraised--not from the standpoint of whether one is getting or is likely to get what one wants--but for their power to nurture. The philosophy of Machiavellianism, so preferred by narcissistic givers, will not be substituted for the practice of honestly negotiating and endeavoring to work through substantive relational differences. While satisfactions are, of course, sought, their attainment tends to be deferred and the pleasures they bring are more likely to be the aftermath rather than the immediate aim of the interaction. This is because there will be what Bion has referred to as the capacity to tolerate frustration, normal depression and the pain intrinsic to emotional development.

An intimate transaction, therefore, is never the product of a hunger for overstimulation, suspense or immediate gratification, the kind of hunger which is regularly fed by televised daytime soap operas. Instead, it finds its gratifications typically in meaningful discovery, developmental unfolding and a cohesive sense of process.

Yet, if it is true that it is the element of intimacy in a human relationship that ultimately most deeply satisfies, why is it, as I have tried to show, that so much narcissistic giving abounds? The answer, I believe, as I wrote at the end of the very first chapter, is that "it is easier to become involved in a relationship that similarly promises short-term gratifications and predictable, swiftly attainable pleasures than to try to cope with and to pursue the elusive, generally delayed, far more risky--but for that reason incomparably more profound, satisfying and even entertaining--rewards intrinsic to the type of human bonding characterized by intimacy."

The great psychoanalyst, D. W. Winnicott, once said that "moral education is no substitute for love". To which you can add that the technique of intimacy, whether as practiced by the mental health profession or by the individual who is looking for a short cut, is no substitute for intimacy.

Yet, as I wrote in *The Singles Scene* (Alper, 1994), "every psychotherapist and student of human nature has seen instances of true intimacy and intimate giving and knows that it exists (otherwise, there would be no point in writing this book). It is important that it occurs, and when it does--even if the final outcome is not a happy one providing the expected gratifications--there are few who do not feel that all the effort and the trouble were well worth it and that the process itself was inherently enriching."

References

Alper, G. 1992 *Portrait of the Artist as a Young Patient. Psychodynamic studies of the creative personality.* New York: Insight Books, Plenum Press. 1994. *The Singles Scene: A Psychoanalytic Study of the Breakdown of Intimacy.* San Francisco: International Scholars Publications.

Balint, Michael 1968 *The Basic Fault.* London: Tavistock Publications, Ltd.

Bion, W. R. 1992 Cogitations. London: H. Karnac Books Ltd.

Erikson, E. M. 1959 *Identity and the life Cycle.* Psychological Issues, No. 1, New York: International Universities Press.

Fenichel, O. 1945 *The Psychoanalytic Theory of Neurosis.* New York: W.W. Norton & Co.

Freud, S. 1915 *Mourning and Melancholia.* Standard Edition 14, 239.

Gleick, J. 1992 *Genius.* New York: Random House.

Goffman, E. 1959 *The Presentation of Self in Everyday Life.* New York: Doubleday.

Joyce, J. 1934 *Ulysses.* New York: Random House.

Kohut, H. 1971 *The Analysis of the Self.* New York: International Universities Press.

Laing, R. D. 1982 *The Voice of Experience.* New York: Pantheon Books.

Langs, R. 1976 *The Therapeutic Interaction.* Vols. 1 & 2. New York: Jason Aronson.

Lorenz, K. 1981 *The Foundations of Ethology.* New York: Simon and Schuster.

Malcolm, J. 1980 *The Impossible Profession.* New York: Random House.

Masson, J. M. 1988 *Against Therapy, Emotional Tyranny and the Myth of Psychological Healing.* New York: Atheneum.

Mayr, E. 1982 *The Growth of Biological Thought.* Cambridge: The Belknap Press of Harvard University Press.

Miller, A. 1981 *The Drama of the Gifted Child.* New York: Basic Books.

Shapiro, D. 1965 *Neurotic Styles.* New York: Basic Books.

Szasz, T. 1959 *The Myth of Mental Illness: Foundations of a Theory of Personal Conduct.* New York: Harper Brothers.

Vonnegut, K. 1965 *God Bless You, Mr. Rosewater.* New York: Dell.

Winnicott, D. W. 1965 *The Maturational Processes and the Facilitating Environment.* New York: International Universities Press, Inc.